CRACKLE GLASS

Identification & Value Guide

Stan & Arlene Weitman

COLLECTOR BOOKS

A Division of Schroeder Publishing Co., Inc.

The current values in this book should be used only as a guide. They are not intended to set prices, which vary from one section of the country to another. Auction prices as well as dealer prices vary greatly and are affected by condition as well as demand. Neither the Authors nor the Publisher assumes responsibility for any losses that might be incurred as a result of consulting this guide.

Searching For A Publisher?

We are always looking for knowledgeable people considered to be experts within their fields. If you feel that there is a real need for a book on your collectible subject and have a large comprehensive collection, contact us.

Cover Design: Beth Summers
Book Design: Benjamin R. Faust

Additional copies of this book may be ordered from:

COLLECTOR BOOKS
P.O. Box 3009
Paducah, KY 42002-3009

-or-

STAN & ARLENE WEITMAN
P.O. Box 1186
N. Massapequa, New York 11758

@ $19.95. Add $2.00 for postage and handling.

Dedication

To our families for their love and support.

To "Poppo" for his never ending encour-

agement and for teaching us to believe in

ourselves.

Acknowledgments

Researching crackle glass was one of the most exciting experiences of our lives. When we went to West Virginia, we met some of the most wonderful people.

Robert McKeand of Pilgrim Glass shared his first-hand knowledge with us. He is an expert in his field. We were truly impressed with his knowledge of not only Pilgrim's crackle glass, but that of other glass blowing companies as well. We thank you, Robert, for being there for us when we visited and every time we called with a page of questions. We will always cherish the rare Voglesong crackle piece that you gave us.

Richard Blenko, Jane McMahon, and Vivian Pridemore also contributed much information, enabling us to write this book. We really appreciate all of you taking time out of your busy schedules and receiving our many calls, especially when we called with last-minute questions. We thank you and all of the Blenko employees for letting us take over the office photostat machine enabling us to copy all of your old catalogs.

We must also thank Robert and Donald Hamon of Hamon Glass. They didn't just tell us how they used to make crackle glass, they showed us. They made us the most beautiful crackle cruet right before our very eyes. You can see them making our cruet on pages 14, 15, and 16.

Last but not least, we would also like to thank our dear friends, Virginia Stone and Carmine Monteforte of Bayvillage Gardens & Antiques, located at 566 Broadway, Route 110, Amityville, Long Island, New York, who encouraged us to take on this endeavor, and who were always there for us.

We would also like to thank the following special people:

Roy Elmer of Vagabond House of Fine Collectibles of West Virginia;

The Corning Museum of Glass;

Eason Eige, Curator of the Huntington Museum;

Caroll Connors, Curator of Ceredo Museum of Ceredo, West Virginia;

Don Walker of the Blenko Glass Company;

Hester McKeand;

Robyn, Jason, and Charlie; and

The *unknown lady*, who sold us our very first crackle cruet at the Commack Flea Market.

Contents

Introduction

About five years ago, we were in a flea market in Commack, Long Island, New York. A woman was inspecting a green cruet made of crackle glass. We heard the vendor ask the customer, "Would you give me three dollars for this cruet?" The customer answered, "No." We immediately stepped forward and said, "We will take the cruet for three dollars." That was it. We were hooked!

We think crackle glass is absolutely beautiful. You would too if you saw it in a window when the sun refracts and reflects off the cracks. A window decorated with different colored crackle glass is truly breathtaking. Five years later, we have a collection in the area of six hundred pieces. We go to tag sales, garage sales, flea markets, auctions, and antique shops. We have even advertised in the paper, sent out circulars, and had crackle business cards made — anything to obtain crackle glass.

Our only problem was that we could find very little information about crackle glass. We discovered there were no books written on our much loved subject. Antique dealers we came into contact with knew less than we did, and expressed a great desire to learn more about this beautiful, fascinating glass. We then decided with the encouragement of our friends, Ginger and Carmine of Bayvillage Gardens & Antiques in Amityville, Long Island, to research and write our very own book, the first book on crackle glass.

Our book consists of pictures and descriptions of crackle items along with a price guide that will greatly help people interested in collecting or selling crackle glass. It will also give a history of where, how, and why crackle glass was developed.

In doing our research, we knew we had to go to West Virginia to obtain the answers to our many unanswered questions. We learned that there were approximately 500 companies creating crackle glass from the late 1930s to early 1970s. Some people even blew crackle glass, as a hobby, in their garages. Also, many companies had workers who went from one company to the next, creating the same or similar pieces. It was therefore impossible for us to identify the creator of each piece. Unless, of course, a piece had a label on it stating its origin. Fortunately, with the help of Robert McKeand, an employee of Pilgrim Glass Corporation for 35 years, and his Pilgrim catalogs, and our Blenko catalogs, supplied to us by Jane McMahon and Vivian Pridemore, we were able to identify the origin of certain pieces. We apologize in advance if we gave a company credit for another company's work.

Dating the pieces was also difficult, as some pieces stayed in the production line for several years after introduction (Pilgrim Glass made the same styles from 1949 to 1969). Again, if possible, we have dated the pieces we could from our catalogs and our visits to the Pilgrim Glass Corporation, Blenko Glass Company, and Ceredo Museum in Ceredo, West Virginia.

In purchasing our crackle glass, we have discovered that the price of crackle glass can vary widely from one part of the country to the next. A piece we had paid $15.00 for in New York, where we live, had an asking price of $95.00 in Pennsylvania. Needless to say, we did not buy the piece in Pennsylvania. Only you as the buyer can decide what you are willing to pay. The same is true for the seller of the piece. Only you as the seller can decide on what you are willing to let a piece go for. Use our price list only as a guide. The buyer and seller are the ones involved in the transaction and determine the worth of a piece.

When pricing our collection, we took into account the rarity and color of each piece. The prices are retail prices for items that are in mint condition. The prices increase on rare items, such as our ladle and punch bowl set and our Voglesong cigarette holder and ashtray on pages 146 and 147. The color smoke (gray) was made only for a short time (early 1950s to 1960s). The number of pieces in this color was limited, thus raising their value. Different colors were and are more expensive to make, such as cranberry, ruby red, amberina, and cobalt blue (amberina is Blenko's tangerine color); therefore, the price reflects this cost. Even though amethyst did not cost more to make than amber or green, it is more collectible today, and therefore warrants a higher price. We will tell you in the chemical composition section on page 12 what chemicals were used to make the different colors.

As you will note, pieces obtained with labels on them demand a higher price, because people would immediately take the labels off and wash the piece. Therefore, it is very hard to find a piece that survived the years with an original label still attached.

Furthermore, a piece with a stopper is more valuable because the stopper took additional hours and manpower to make. Also, the same person who made the cruet did not necessarily make the stopper. In addition, stoppers were very fragile and many did not survive the passage of time.

Crackle glass is still being made today by the Blenko Glass Company. Other countries abroad, such as Taiwan and China, are presently producing crackle glass in the form of drinking glasses and vases, just to name a few. Old crackle glass is highly collectible today; new crackle glass may be collectible tomorrow.

Make sure you check the pieces when purchasing crackle glass to see that they are in good condition; that they are not chipped or cracked (even though it is called crackle glass). We have made the mistake many times, in purchasing a piece of glass, being over-zealous, not carefully checking the piece, and thinking we had a great buy, only to go home and see the piece was defective. Any defects will automatically devalue the piece. We suggest you hold the piece up to the light and turn it slowly in all directions to see if there are any imperfections. Make sure your piece is properly wrapped to protect it until you get home.

The Manufacturers of Crackle Glass

The exact origin of crackle glass is unknown. The sixteenth century Venetian glassmakers claimed credit for the procedure of plunging red-hot glass into cold water, and then reheating and reblowing it. This technique produced glass that appeared to be covered with multiple fractures, but the interior surfaces remained smooth to the touch. Neighboring Bohemian glassmakers, it is written, copied this technique, and it became popular throughout Europe.

Martin Bach of the Durand Glass Factory in the United States claimed that in 1928, he manufactured Egyptian and Moorish Art Nouveau glass that were reproductions of crackle glass from those ancient civilizations. We will never know who made the first crackle glass. What we do know, however, is that from the late 1930s to the early 1970s crackle glass was produced in abundance, especially in the earlier days when over 500 companies were making it in the West Virginia area. West Virginia was known as "Glass Country." Many glass companies set up their operations in this region because they were afforded the geographical advantage of having the greatest abundance of natural gas for commercial use.

Some of the companies, who we know, that made crackle during that period are: Pilgrim Glass Corporation, Blenko Glass Company, Hamon Glass Company, Bischoff Glass Company, Kanawha Glass Company, Voglesong Glass Company, Mt. Washington Glass Company, Viking Glass Company, Williamsburg Glass Company, Rainbow Glass Company, and Cambridge Glass Company. Some of these companies are still operating today. Blenko is the only one of the above-named companies that is still making crackle glass. Fenton Glass Company located in Williamstown, West Virginia, started making crackle glass in the early 1990s, but discontinued making it a few years ago.

When we asked Mr. McKeand of Pilgrim Glass Corporation why so many of the glass blowing companies went out of business, he said, "American hand-made glass flourished up until the year of 1940 when Central Glass of Willy, Virginia, went out of business. World War II helped the American economy because you could not get glass from Europe because of the war. In this modern era, many glass factories have gone out of business. In 1990, the last statistic showed that American-made glass sells only eight percent of the market. Imports have a ninety-two percent market share."

We were fortunate to visit three glass factories that are in existence today in West Virginia, who made crackle from the late 1930s to the early 1970s. They are: The Pilgrim Glass Corporation, Blenko Glass Company, and Hamon Glass Company (Blenko Glass Company still produces a few crackle pieces today). They shared the history of their companies with us. In addition, they were able to tell us the histories of other glass makers who are no longer in operation today.

History of Crackle Glass Companies

Pilgrim Glass Corporation

A history of the Pilgrim Glass Corporation was supplied to us by Robert McKeand in his article, "The Pilgrim Glass Corporation," April, 1993.

"In the later 1940s Walter Bailey was operating a small glass factory on Michigan Street in the Westmoreland section of Huntington, West Virginia. Since the company was small and not making much progress, Mr. Bailey decided to sell.

"Alfred E. Knobler, a Ceramic Engineer, was buying most of the glass the factory was making, and he purchased what was then Tri-State Glass Mfg. from Mr. Bailey. Mr. Knobler had no room to expand the facilities and began looking for a suitable place to build a new factory. He found a suitable area on Walkers Branch Road in Ceredo, West Virginia, and purchased the ground from Mr. Golden Ramey. The new facility opened in 1956.

"The main items the factory produced from 1949 until 1970 were crackled glass in Ruby, Tangerine, Amethyst, Smoke, Sapphire, Amber, Green, and Crystal."

To our knowledge, unlike other companies, Pilgrim changed the colors of their labels. The changes were as follows: The yellow label was the first; black; white and silver; black, blue, and white; and now black and white.

One way to definitely identify a Pilgrim piece is by a strawberry mark on the bottom of the piece. This was done by the blower hitting the bottom of the glass with a file while the glass was still hot and soft (See page 111, close-up of Plate 282). Not all the Pilgrim pieces have the strawberry mark, however.

If you are in the West Virginia area, you must see Robert McKeand's crackle collection which is on display at the Pilgrim Glass Corporation and the Ceredo Museum at 501 Main Street, Ceredo, West Virginia, 25507.

The Pilgrim Glass Corporation is located in Ceredo, West Virginia, 25507. You can call them at (304)453-3553.

Blenko Glass Company

"The founder of Blenko Glass Company, William J. Blenko (1855 – 1933) came to American from London in the early 1890s for one purpose, to produce in this country handblown glass for use in stained glass windows. In 1929 handblown decorative glassware started to be produced and eventually used by such people as Eleanor Roosevelt and Mamie Eisenhower. Blenko continues to make such glass, producing it in hundreds of individual colors for use by artists whose field is stained glass. The tradition of handmade glassware is continued by the third and fourth generations of the Blenko Family."

Blenko started crackling in the 1930s, and is still producing crackle today in the form of fish, rose bowls, drinking glasses, hurricane-shade tops, and a few large bowls. Blenko prides themselves in the fact that they used rosettes to decorate some of their pieces. The rosettes were made by hand, and put on by the blower and sometimes the finisher. In 1959 and 1960, Blenko sandblasted their name on their pieces. This was done because Blenko was trying to patent all their shapes. It had the word Blenko with a little hand under it. You might, and we say might, find pieces of Blenko with the signatures of Richard Blenko or his father or his grandfather, and these would be highly collectible and rare. Also, the designers have signed a few pieces. Blenko Glass was and still is known for its large pieces, some reaching over 23 inches in length.

"The factory attracts thousands of visitors from the U.S. and the world over. Here they can watch the molten glass take form as Blenko craftsmen practice their skilled art." (Blenko Glass Booklet) Crackle glass and other historic glass is on display in the Blenko Museum.

Blenko is located in Milton, West Virginia. You can contact them at (304)743-9081.

Hamon Glass

In our interview with Robert Hamon, he told us that Hamon Glass was established in 1932. He stated that he started glass blowing at the age of ten. He used to be a consultant to the Kanawha Glass Company and taught the art of glass making to the Pilgrim Glass Company. Hamon Glass started blowing crackle glass in the late 1940s. In 1966, Hamon Glass merged with the Kanawha Glass Company, each keeping its own name and glass blowing technique. Please keep this in mind when reading our identification section, as some pieces identified as Kanawha may have been in fact created by Hamon Glass. If you find a piece with a Kanawha label on it, and it has a pontil mark and no visible seams, it was most probably made by Hamon Glass. Robert Hamon told us his company made pieces for Kanawha that were later featured in the Kanawha catalogs. Robert Hamon also told us that his company made crackle glass for the "T.V. Trading Stamp Company." Hamon Glass stopped making crackle in the mid 1970s because there was no more demand for it. The company is presently manufacturing paperweights, blown glass and glass sculptures, and glass marbles. Robert and his wife Veronica are a glass-sculpting team, who create visual masterpieces.

Hamon Glass is located at 102 Hamon Road, Scott Depot, West Virginia. (304)757-9067.

Kanawha Glass Company

Kanawha Glass Company was located in Dunbar, West Virginia. It was established in 1957, and produced crackle up until 1987 when they went out of business. It was owned by the Meritt family. All of the crackle pieces from Kanawha have smooth bottoms.

Voglesong Glass Company

Voglesong Glass Company operated in Huntington, West Virginia, from 1949 to 1951. Since they only made crackle for two years, any piece found would be very valuable (See page 146, Plate 378).

Rainbow Art Glass Company

We could not find much about Rainbow Art Glass Company because the factory burned down in the 1960s. We do know that they were making crackle up until that time. Rainbow was reorganized as the Rainbow Art Glass Company, a division of Viking Glass Company in Huntington, West Virginia. When the company went out of business, the Rainbow name was bought by an employee, and now is operated as Rainbow Glass, Inc. It is located at Route 3, Box 43, Proctorville, Ohio, 45669.

Bischoff Glass Company

The Bischoff Glass Company was founded in Huntington, West Virginia, in 1922, on Jackson Avenue. Sometime in the 1940s they moved to Culloden, West Virginia. They operated until 1963, when Lois Bischoff sold the factory to Lancaster Colony. They continued operation until about 1968, when they sold it to Chuck Sloan. They made lighting glass. Crackle glass was made from 1942 to 1963.

The Process of Making Crackle Glass

No two people were more surprised than we were when we discovered one of the main reasons crackle glass was produced. We always thought this beautiful glass, made in every vibrant color imaginable, was created to decorate and enhance a room or window. We found out this was true, but imagine our surprise when we were told that crackle glass was also made to cover up imperfections in the glass.

When a piece of glass was found to be corded, having a heavy line or swirl in the glass (a different composition or characteristic than the main body of the glass) after it is blown and shaped, it would not be a high-quality piece, as the different characteristic would become an imperfection. Therefore, crackle glass became commonplace in the glass blowing factories to cover up imperfections in the glass. In our interview with Mr. Hamon, he stated, "If you were making plain glass, and one had a cord in it, you crackled it, you covered it up, and that is why everybody made crackle glass."

Having over six hundred pieces in our personal collection, we see that each one has a personality of its own. Even when you have two pieces that are the same style and color, and are made by the same factory, they are unique in their own way. For instance, we have two tangerine (amberina) Blenko decanters, which look identical, but with close inspection, you will notice that they are in fact very different. One has a smaller opening, which would inhibit the switching of stoppers from one to the other, and one has a definite tilt to it. This is due, we feel, to the fact that glass blowers are not just highly skilled craftsmen, but also talented artists. Their own experience and creativity go into each piece of glass they make.

There are several ways these artists made crackle glass. All are different, and all produce a different effect.

The first method was to take a hot glob of glass attached to the end of a blow pipe and dip it into cold water. The glob of glass would instantly crackle. If the glob of glass was of a bigger size it would take a little longer to crackle, even though the process of crackling was quick. The thicker the glass the larger the cracks. After the glob of glass crackled, the glass blower would insert the crackled glob back into the glory hole (oven) and reheat it, thereby resealing the cracks. He would then remove it and blow the piece and shape it to the desired style. This method of crackling always produced a large crackle, because as the glass was blown, it would expand and the cracks would get larger.

The second method was to heat the glob of glass and blow the desired style and then immerse it into cold water. The shaped piece would crackle and then be put back into the glory hole to be reheated and to seal the cracks. This method also always produced large cracks.

The third method was a little different than the first two. To make the glass crackle finer, you would roll the piece into sawdust before plunging it into water. The sawdust forms a carbon, the carbon then protects the piece of glass from being viciously attacked with deeper cracks. Mr. Hamon, of Hamon Glass said, "We rolled every one of our pieces of crackle in sawdust so we could get the finer cracks. Blowing the glass into a shape and then crackling it was a better method than crackling the glob of glass first and reheating it, and then blowing it into a shape." Robert McKeand from Pilgrim Glass stated, "This method produced an 'onion crackle.'" Pilgrim Glass and Hamon Glass used this method.

The fourth method was called the hot-mold process. Kanawha was known for using this method. Hot molten glass was blown into a metal mold. The metal mold was kept preheated so the sides would be nice and slick. The piece would be held in one spot, causing seams on opposite sides of the piece. The bottoms of the Kanawha molded pieces were always smooth, as every metal mold has a bottom plate on it. There was never a pontil rod attached, so there was never a need to finish the already smooth bottoms.

The fifth method was used by Hamon Glass when they created their molded pieces. They blew their glass into a metal mold that was not hot. The mold, which was called a paste mold was lined with paste and cork. The corking made the inside of the mold slick. The blower kept turning the piece inside the mold, round and round, which in turn eliminated seam marks. Hamon Glass always put a pontil mark on their molded pieces. Mr. Hamon told us that molded pieces were much faster to produce.

You may find a piece of crackle that has very small, fine cracks and big cracks. Where the big cracks are, sawdust was never applied. It is important to note that the bigger cracked pieces are of equal value to the smaller, finer cracked pieces.

On the following pages, you will see photographs of Robert Hamon making a crackle cruet.

Crackle glass is known for its vibrant colors. Each of the companies that we interviewed had different names for their colors, even though they may have been the same color. For instance, the combination of orange and yellow, red and orange, and red and yellow were commonly known as amberina. Blenko calls these combinations tangerine, whereas, Pilgrim's tangerine was orange.

Throughout the years Blenko has made over 1,300 different colors. Every few years Blenko came out with either new colors or different color names for their already existing colors. According to our Blenko book (1930 – 1953) and with the help of Vivian Pridemore of Blenko, we found that the following colors were in production during the late 1930s through the late 1970s: tangerine, amber, emerald green, topaz, ruby, deep sapphire, sapphire, deep amethyst, light amethyst, cobalt, citron, pale green, turqoise, antique green, light blue, light green, deep amber, chartreuse, violet, sea green, marine crystal, sky blue, jonquil (yellow), Persian (midnight blue), crystal, charcoal, lemon, olive green, wheat, graff (green), and charisma (crystal orange swirl).

From 1949 to 1969 Pilgrim crackle pieces were also available in an assortment of many beautiful and intense colors. You will note that we dated our Pilgrim pieces from 1949 to 1969, because the Pilgrim styles and colors changed very little from year to year. We do know that amberina was introduced by Pilgrim in 1949.

Crystal handles came to be in the early 1960s and smoke gray showed itself for a very brief time in the 1950s. Also, rose crystal had a short life, as Pilgrim stopped producing it because there was little demand for that particular color. The Pilgrim decorator shades are: amethyst, sea green, sky blue, tangerine (orange), topaz (light amber), lemon lime, ruby, amberina, olive green, crystal, smoke gray, and amber (brown).

We were fortunate to receive from the Hamon Glass Company a list of some of their crackle colors along with the chemical composition of these colors. They were as follows:

<u>Yellow</u>
Titinium
Cerium

<u>Dark Green</u>
Red Iron
Black Copper
Chrome Oxide

<u>Amber</u>
Oats (Western) Brown Sugar
Sulphur
Selenium
Manganese

<u>Dark Blue</u>
Black Oxide of Copper
Cobalt

<u>Amethyst</u>
Manganese

<u>Ruby (Amberina)</u>
Sulphur
Selenium
Cadium

NOTE: the longer you keep a piece of glass made from this chemical composition, in the glory hole, the darker it would get. If it is kept in too long the red would turn black.

<u>Orange</u>
Cadmium
Selenium

It is interesting to note that glass is a liquid solid. When sand is heated to a very high temperature, about 2,600°, it melts. It is worked at about 2,100°. When the liquid cools it becomes glass. Before melting, other ingredients (soda ash and limestone) were added to the sand to give it an infinite variation in the quality of the finished glass. Soda, when added, lowers the melting point of the glass batch, but at the same time makes a soft glass lacking in strength. The limestone was a stabilizer. It would harden, making it easier to work the molten glass. Crystal glass would result from these basic materials. If a colored glass was desired, the chemicals added to the basic material batch would result in a particular color.

PLATE 1. The Hamon Glass Building.

PLATE 2. Mr. Robert Hamon holding a crackle pitcher made in the 1950s.

PLATE 3. The glory hole reaching temperatures of 2,800°.

PLATE 4. A hot glob of glass attached to the blow pipe in the first stages of being blown.

PLATE 5. Slightly cooling the glass to be blown into the desired shape. (In the background are a number of blowpipes of different sizes that are used in blowing glass. In the foreground are different tools that are used in shaping the glass and cutting of the glass.)

PLATE 6. The immersion of the hot glass into water.

PLATE 7. Shaping the neck of the cruet.

PLATE 8. Attaching the pontil to the bottom of the cruet.

PLATE 9. Cutting the blowpipe from the cruet.

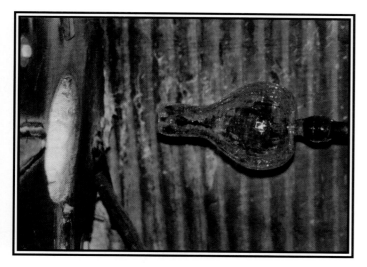

PLATE 10. Placing the cruet back into the glory hole to seal all cracks.

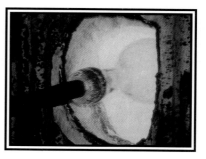

PLATE 11. In the glory hole.

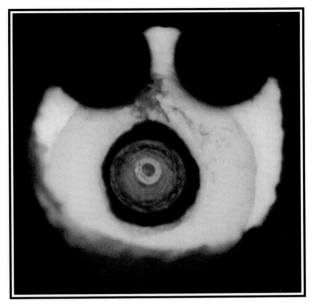

PLATE 12. Looking inside the glory hole from the opposite side.

PLATE 13. Applying a handle to the cruet.

PLATE 14. Shaping the handle.

PLATE 15. Handle fully shaped.

PLATE 16. The finished cruet. This cruet was the first piece of crackle glass that Mr. Hamon has blown in twenty-five years. This cruet was signed by Robert & Donald Hamon and given to us as a gift. We were not able to take it home right away. The cruet had to cool for several days. It was placed in a cool-down oven, as all blown glass is. Mr. Hamon also made a stopper for this cruet and the cruet was shipped to us several days later. We will always treasure this cruet.

Pitchers and Cruets

PLATE 17. A pitcher is a container with a spout or lip and a handle used for holding liquids to be poured.

PLATE 18
HEIGHT: 3½"
COLOR: Amberina
STYLE: Miniature Pitcher
HANDLE: Drop over
COMPANY: Pilgrim
DATE: 1949 – 1969
VALUE: $30.00 – $35.00
REMARKS: Note close-up picture
           of drop over handle.

Close-up of Plate 18.

PLATE 19
HEIGHT: 3½"
COLOR: Tangerine
STYLE: Miniature Pitcher
HANDLE: Drop over
COMPANY: Pilgrim
DATE: 1949 – 1969
VALUE: $30.00 – $35.00

PLATE 20
HEIGHT: 3¼"
COLOR: Amethyst
STYLE: Miniature Pitcher
HANDLE: Drop over
COMPANY: Pilgrim
DATE: 1949 – 1969
VALUE: $35.00 – $40.00
REMARKS: Amethyst is a highly
            collectible color and
            warrants a higher price.

PLATE 21
HEIGHT: 3¾"
COLOR: Topaz
STYLE: Miniature Pitcher
HANDLE: Drop over
COMPANY: Pilgrim
DATE: 1949 – 1969
VALUE: $25.00 – $30.00

PLATE 22
HEIGHT: 4"
COLOR: Emerald Green
STYLE: Miniature Pitcher
HANDLE: Drop over
COMPANY: Pilgrim
DATE: 1949 – 1969
VALUE: $25.00 – $30.00

PLATE 23
HEIGHT: 3¾"
COLOR: Amberina
STYLE: Miniature Pitcher
HANDLE: Drop over
COMPANY: Pilgrim
DATE: 1949 – 1969
VALUE: $30.00 – $35.00

PLATE 24
HEIGHT: 3¼"
COLOR: Ruby
STYLE: Miniature Pitcher
HANDLE: Drop over
COMPANY: Pilgrim
DATE: 1949 – 1969
VALUE: $30.00 – $35.00

PLATE 25
HEIGHT: 3⅛"
COLOR: Tangerine
STYLE: Miniature Pitcher
HANDLE: Drop over
COMPANY: Pilgrim
DATE: 1949 – 1969
VALUE: $30.00 – $35.00

PLATE 26
HEIGHT: 3¼"
COLOR: Olive Green
STYLE: Miniature Pitcher
HANDLE: Drop over
COMPANY: Pilgrim
DATE: 1949 – 1969
VALUE: $30.00 – $40.00
REMARKS: Left-handed, rare. Note location of spout.

PLATE 27
HEIGHT: 3¾"
COLOR: Topaz
STYLE: Miniature Pitcher
HANDLE: Drop over
COMPANY: Pilgrim
DATE: 1949 – 1969
VALUE: $25.00 – $30.00

PLATE 28
HEIGHT: 3¾"
COLOR: Amberina
STYLE: Miniature Pitcher
HANDLE: Drop over
COMPANY: Pilgrim
DATE: 1949 – 1969
VALUE: $30.00 – $35.00

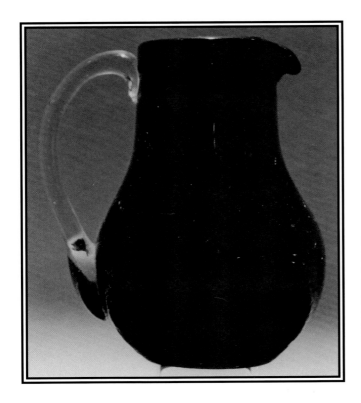

PLATE 29
HEIGHT: 3¾"
COLOR: Tangerine
STYLE: Miniature Pitcher
HANDLE: Drop over
COMPANY: Pilgrim
DATE: 1949 – 1969
VALUE: $30.00 – $35.00

PLATE 30
HEIGHT: 4"
COLOR: Dark Amber
STYLE: Miniature Pitcher
HANDLE: Drop over
COMPANY: Pilgrim
DATE: 1949 – 1969
VALUE: $25.00 – $30.00

PLATE 31
HEIGHT: 3½"
COLOR: Ruby
STYLE: Miniature Pitcher
HANDLE: Drop over
COMPANY: Pilgrim
DATE: 1949 – 1969
VALUE: $30.00 – $35.00

PLATE 32
HEIGHT: 3¾"
COLOR: Ruby
STYLE: Miniature Pitcher
HANDLE: Drop over
COMPANY: Pilgrim
DATE: 1949 – 1969
VALUE: $30.00 – $35.00

PLATE 33
HEIGHT: 3¾"
COLOR: Lemon Lime
STYLE: Miniature Pitcher
HANDLE: Drop over
COMPANY: Pilgrim
DATE: 1949 – 1969
VALUE: $25.00 – $30.00

PLATE 34
HEIGHT: 3¾"
COLOR: Ruby
STYLE: Pitcher
HANDLE: Drop over
COMPANY: Pilgrim
DATE: 1949 – 1969
VALUE: $30.00 – $35.00

PLATE 35
HEIGHT: 3¾"
COLOR: Amberina
STYLE: Miniature Pitcher
HANDLE: Drop over
COMPANY: Pilgrim
DATE: 1949 – 1969
VALUE: $30.00 – $35.00

PLATE 36
HEIGHT: 3¾"
COLOR: Tangerine
STYLE: Miniature Pitcher
HANDLE: Drop over
COMPANY: Pilgrim
DATE: 1949 – 1969
VALUE: $40.00 – $45.00
REMARKS: Left-handed. Note location of spout

PLATE 37
HEIGHT: 4"
COLOR: Tangerine
STYLE: Miniature Pitcher
HANDLE: Pulled back
COMPANY: Pilgrim
DATE: 1949 – 1969
VALUE: $30.00 – $35.00
REMARKS: Note close-up picture of pulled back handle.

Close-up of Plate 37.

PLATE 38
HEIGHT: 4¼"
COLOR: Lemon Lime
STYLE: Miniature Pitcher
HANDLE: Pulled back
COMPANY: Pilgrim
DATE: 1949 – 1969
VALUE: $25.00 – $30.00

PLATE 39
HEIGHT: 3"
COLOR: Ruby
STYLE: Miniature Pitcher Set
HANDLE: Pulled back
COMPANY: Unknown
DATE: Unknown
VALUE: $60.00 – $70.00 (set)

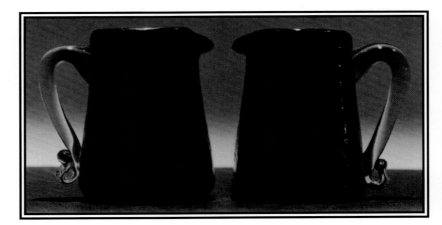

PLATE 40
HEIGHT: 4"
COLOR: Ruby
STYLE: Miniature Pitcher
HANDLE: Pulled back
COMPANY: Pilgrim
DATE: 1949 – 1969
VALUE: $30.00 – $35.00

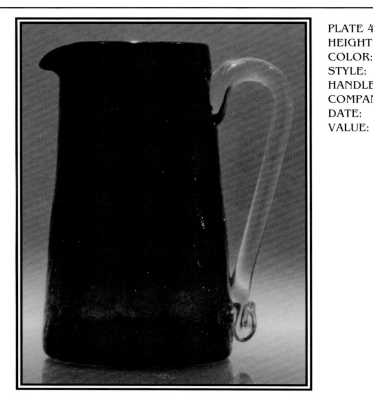

PLATE 41
HEIGHT: 3¾"
COLOR: Tangerine
STYLE: Miniature Pitcher
HANDLE: Pulled back
COMPANY: Pilgrim
DATE: 1949 – 1969
VALUE: $30.00 – $35.00

PLATE 42
HEIGHT: 4"
COLOR: Blue
STYLE: Miniature Pitcher
HANDLE: Pulled back
COMPANY: Pilgrim
DATE: 1949 – 1969
VALUE: $25.00 – $30.00

Close-up of Plate 43.

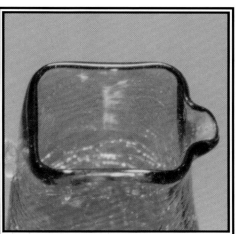

PLATE 43
HEIGHT: 4"
COLOR: Blue
STYLE: Miniature Pitcher
HANDLE: Drop over
COMPANY: Unknown
DATE: Unknown
VALUE: $40.00 – $45.00
REMARKS: Square opening (close-up).

PLATE 44
HEIGHT: 3¾"
COLOR: Tangerine
STYLE: Miniature Pitcher
HANDLE: Drop over
COMPANY: Pilgrim
DATE: 1949 – 1969
VALUE: $30.00 – $35.00

PLATE 45
HEIGHT: 3½"
COLOR: Olive Green
STYLE: Miniature Pitcher
HANDLE: Drop over
COMPANY: Pilgrim
DATE: 1949 – 1969
VALUE: $25.00 – $30.00

PLATE 46
HEIGHT: 3½"
COLOR: Gold
STYLE: Miniature Pitcher
HANDLE: Drop over
COMPANY: Rainbow
DATE: Late 1940s – 1960s
VALUE: $25.00 – $30.00

PLATE 47
HEIGHT: 3¾"
COLOR: Topaz
STYLE: Miniature Pitcher
HANDLE: Drop over
COMPANY: Unknown
DATE: Unknown
VALUE: $25.00 – $30.00

PLATE 48
HEIGHT: 3½"
COLOR: Ruby
STYLE: Miniature Pitcher
HANDLE: Drop over
COMPANY: Pilgrim
DATE: 1949 – 1969
VALUE: $30.00 – $35.00

Close-up of Plate 49.

PLATE 49
HEIGHT: 3¾"
COLOR: Topaz
STYLE: Miniature Pitcher
HANDLE: Ribbed, crystal drop over
COMPANY: Pilgrim
DATE: 1949 – 1969
VALUE: $35.00 – $40.00
REMARKS: Ribbed handle pieces are priced higher.

PLATE 50
HEIGHT: 3½"
COLOR: Green
STYLE: Miniature Pitcher
HANDLE: Drop over
COMPANY: Pilgrim
DATE: 1949 – 1969
VALUE: $25.00 – $30.00

PLATE 51
HEIGHT: 3½"
COLOR: Green
STYLE: Miniature Pitcher
HANDLE: Drop over
COMPANY: Pilgrim
DATE: 1949 – 1969
VALUE: $35.00 – $40.00
REMARKS: Left handed. Note location of spout.

PLATE 52
HEIGHT: 3¼"
COLOR: Green
STYLE: Miniature Pitcher
HANDLE: Pulled back
COMPANY: Kanawha/Hamon
DATE: 1966 – 1970s
VALUE: $35.00 – $40.00
REMARKS: Labels increase the price. Hamon and
             Kanawha merged in 1966. This is a
             Hamon piece even though it has a
             Kanawha label.

PLATE 53
HEIGHT: 3¼"
COLOR: Topaz
STYLE: Miniature Pitcher
HANDLE: Pulled back
COMPANY: Hamon
DATE: 1966 – 1970s
VALUE: $25.00 – $30.00

PLATE 54
HEIGHT: 3¼"
COLOR: Topaz
STYLE: Miniature Pitcher
HANDLE: Pulled back
COMPANY: Hamon
DATE: 1966 – 1970s
VALUE: $25.00 – $30.00

PLATE 55
HEIGHT: 3¼"
COLOR: Amberina
STYLE: Miniature Pitcher
HANDLE: Drop over
COMPANY: Pilgrim
DATE: 1949 – 1969
VALUE: $30.00 – $35.00

PLATE 56
HEIGHT: 3¼"
COLOR: Sea Green
STYLE: Miniature Pitcher
HANDLE: Drop over
COMPANY: Pilgrim
DATE: 1949 – 1969
VALUE: $25.00 – $30.00
REMARKS: Courtesy of Bayvillage Gardens &
           Antiques, Amityville, Long Island

PLATE 57
HEIGHT: 3½"
COLOR: Olive Green
STYLE: Miniature Pitcher
HANDLE: Drop over
COMPANY: Pilgrim
DATE: 1949 – 1969
VALUE: $25.00 – $30.00

PLATE 58
HEIGHT: 3¼"
COLOR: Crystal
STYLE: Miniature Pitcher
HANDLE: Drop over
COMPANY: Pilgrim
DATE: 1949 – 1969
VALUE: $25.00 – $30.00

PLATE 59
HEIGHT: 3¾"
COLOR: Ruby
STYLE: Miniature Pitcher
HANDLE: Drop over
COMPANY: Pilgrim
DATE: 1949 – 1969
VALUE: $30.00 – $35.00

PLATE 60
HEIGHT: 3¾"
COLOR: Lemon Lime
STYLE: Miniature Pitcher
HANDLE: Drop over
COMPANY: Pilgrim
DATE: 1949 – 1969
VALUE: $25.00 – $30.00

PLATE 61
HEIGHT: 3¾"
COLOR: Sea Green
STYLE: Miniature Pitcher
HANDLE: Drop over
COMPANY: Pilgrim
DATE: 1949 – 1969
VALUE: $25.00 – $30.00

PLATE 62
HEIGHT: 4"
COLOR: Lemon Lime
STYLE: Miniature Pitcher
HANDLE: Drop over
COMPANY: Pilgrim
DATE: 1949 – 1969
VALUE: $25.00 – $30.00

PLATE 63
HEIGHT: 4"
COLOR: Light Amber
STYLE: Miniature Pitcher
HANDLE: Drop over
COMPANY: Pilgrim
DATE: 1949 – 1969
VALUE: $35.00 – $40.00
REMARKS: Left-handed, rare. Note location of spout.

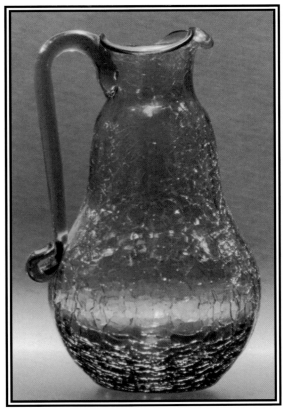

PLATE 64
HEIGHT: 4½"
COLOR: Light Amethyst (Lilac)
STYLE: Miniature Pitcher
HANDLE: Pulled back
COMPANY: Pilgrim
DATE: 1949 – 1969
VALUE: $40.00 – $45.00
REMARKS: Amethyst is a highly collectible color and
            warrants a higher price.

PLATE 65
HEIGHT: 4¼"
COLOR: Tangerine
STYLE: Miniature Pitcher
HANDLE: Drop over
COMPANY: Pilgrim
DATE: 1949 – 1969
VALUE: $30.00 – $35.00

PLATE 66
HEIGHT: 3½"
COLOR: Ruby
STYLE: Miniature Pitcher
HANDLE: Drop over
COMPANY: Pilgrim
DATE: 1949 – 1969
VALUE: $35.00 – $40.00
REMARKS: Frilled top.

PLATE 67
HEIGHT: 3½"
COLOR: Blue
STYLE: Miniature Pitcher
HANDLE: Drop over
COMPANY: Pilgrim
DATE: 1949 – 1969
VALUE: $35.00 – $40.00
REMARKS: Frilled top and odd shaped handle.

PLATE 68
HEIGHT: 3½"
COLOR: Olive Green
STYLE: Miniature Pitcher
HANDLE: Drop over
COMPANY: Pilgrim
DATE: 1949 – 1969
VALUE: $25.00 – $30.00

PLATE 69
HEIGHT: 4¾"
COLOR: Blue
STYLE: Miniature Pitcher
HANDLE: Pulled back
COMPANY: Unknown
DATE: Unknown
VALUE: $45.00 – $50.00

PLATE 70
HEIGHT: 4½"
COLOR: Cobalt
STYLE: Miniature Pitcher
HANDLE: Pulled back
COMPANY: Unknown
DATE: Unknown
VALUE: $60.00 – $65.00
REMARKS: Cobalt demands higher prices.

PLATE 71
HEIGHT: 4½"
COLOR: Light Amber
STYLE: Miniature Pitcher
HANDLE: Pulled back
COMPANY: Unknown
DATE: Unknown
VALUE: $25.00 – $30.00

PLATE 72
HEIGHT: 4½"
COLOR: Ruby
STYLE: Miniature Pitcher
HANDLE: Drop over
COMPANY: Pilgrim
DATE: 1949 – 1969
VALUE: $30.00 – $35.00

PLATE 73
HEIGHT: 4¼"
COLOR: Amethyst
STYLE: Miniature Pitcher
HANDLE: Pulled back
COMPANY: Pilgrim
DATE: 1949 – 1969
VALUE: $40.00 – $45.00
REMARKS: Amethyst is a highly
collectible color and
warrants a higher price.

PLATE 74
HEIGHT: 4½"
COLOR: Olive Green
STYLE: Miniature Pitcher
HANDLE: Pulled Back
COMPANY: Pilgrim
DATE: 1949 – 1969
VALUE: $25.00 – $30.00

PLATE 75
HEIGHT: 4½"
COLOR: Olive Green
STYLE: Miniature Pitcher
HANDLE: Ribbed, crystal drop over
COMPANY: Pilgrim
DATE: 1949 – 1969
VALUE: $35.00 – $40.00
REMARKS: Ribbed handle pieces priced higher.

PLATE 76
HEIGHT: 4¼"
COLOR: Blue
STYLE: Miniature Pitcher
HANDLE: Pulled back
COMPANY: Pilgrim
DATE: 1949 – 1969
VALUE: $25.00 – $30.00

PLATE 77
HEIGHT: 4½"
COLOR: Ruby
STYLE: Miniature Pitcher
HANDLE: Pulled back
COMPANY: Pilgrim
DATE: 1949 – 1969
VALUE: $30.00 – $35.00

PLATE 78
HEIGHT: 4¼"
COLOR: Amberina
STYLE: Miniature Pitcher
HANDLE: Drop over
COMPANY: Pilgrim
DATE: 1949 – 1969
VALUE: $30.00 – $35.00

PLATE 79
HEIGHT: 4¼"
COLOR: Tangerine
STYLE: Miniature Pitcher
HANDLE: Drop over
COMPANY: Pilgrim
DATE: 1949 – 1969
VALUE: $30.00 – $35.00

PLATE 80
HEIGHT: 4½"
COLOR: Amberina
STYLE: Miniature Pitcher
HANDLE: Ribbed, crystal drop over
COMPANY: Pilgrim
DATE: 1949 – 1969
VALUE: $40.00 – $50.00
REMARKS: Ribbed handle pieces priced higher.

PLATE 81
HEIGHT: 4½"
COLOR: Tangerine
STYLE: Miniature Pitcher
HANDLE: Drop over
COMPANY: Pilgrim
DATE: 1949 – 1969
VALUE: $40.00 – $45.00
REMARKS: Frilled top.

PLATE 82
HEIGHT: 4¼"
COLOR: Olive Green
STYLE: Miniature Pitcher
HANDLE: Drop over
COMPANY: Pilgrim
DATE: 1949 – 1969
VALUE: $35.00 – $40.00
REMARKS: Frilled top.

PLATE 83
HEIGHT: 4¼"
COLOR: Blue
STYLE: Miniature Pitcher
HANDLE: Drop over
COMPANY: Pilgrim
DATE: 1949 – 1969
VALUE: $35.00 – $40.00
REMARKS: Frilled top.

PLATE 84
HEIGHT: 4¾"
COLOR: Amberina
STYLE: Miniature Pitcher
HANDLE: Pulled back
COMPANY: Pilgrim
DATE: 1949 – 1969
VALUE: $30.00 – $35.00

PLATE 85
HEIGHT: 4¾"
COLOR: Topaz
STYLE: Miniature Pitcher
HANDLE: Pulled back
COMPANY: Pilgrim
DATE: 1949 – 1969
VALUE: $25.00 – $30.00

PLATE 86
HEIGHT: 4¾"
COLOR: Olive Green
STYLE: Miniature Pitcher
HANDLE: Drop over
COMPANY: Pilgrim
DATE: 1949 – 1969
VALUE: $35.00 – $40.00
REMARKS: Labels increase the price.

PLATE 87
HEIGHT: 5"
COLOR: Olive Green
STYLE: Miniature Pitcher
HANDLE: Ribbed, crystal drop over
COMPANY: Pilgrim
DATE: 1949 – 1969
VALUE: $35.00 – $40.00
REMARKS: Ribbed handle pieces priced higher.
            Courtesy of Bayvillage Gardens &
            Antiques, Amityville, Long Island.

PLATE 88
HEIGHT: 5½"
COLOR: Emerald Green
STYLE: Pitcher
HANDLE: Drop over
COMPANY: Unknown
DATE: Unknown
VALUE: $25.00 – $30.00

PLATE 89
HEIGHT: 5¾"
COLOR: Topaz
STYLE: Pitcher
HANDLE: Drop over
COMPANY: Unknown
DATE: Unknown
VALUE: $25.00 – $30.00

PLATE 90
HEIGHT: 5"
COLOR: Olive Green
STYLE: Miniature Pitcher
HANDLE: Drop over
COMPANY: Pilgrim
DATE: 1949 – 1969
VALUE: $25.00 – $30.00

PLATE 91
HEIGHT: 5"
COLOR: Dark Amber
STYLE: Miniature Pitcher
HANDLE: Drop over
COMPANY: Pilgrim
DATE: 1949 – 1969
VALUE: $25.00 – $30.00

PLATE 92
HEIGHT: 4¼"
COLOR: Dark Amber
STYLE: Miniature Pitcher
HANDLE: Pulled back
COMPANY: Pilgrim
DATE: 1949 – 1969
VALUE: $25.00 – $30.00

PLATE 93
HEIGHT: 5¼"
COLOR: Topaz
STYLE: Pitcher
HANDLE: Drop over
COMPANY: Unknown
DATE: Unknown
VALUE: $30.00 – $35.00
REMARKS: Blown into a mold.

PLATE 94
HEIGHT: 5¼"
COLOR: Emerald Green
STYLE: Pitcher
HANDLE: Drop over
COMPANY: Unknown
DATE: Unknown
VALUE: $30.00 – $35.00
REMARKS: Blown into a mold.

PLATE 95
HEIGHT: 4¼"
COLOR: Cobalt
STYLE: Miniature Pitcher
HANDLE: Pulled back
COMPANY: Unknown
DATE: Unknown
VALUE: $60.00 – $70.00
REMARKS: Cobalt demands
           higher prices.

PLATE 96
HEIGHT: 4½"
COLOR: Ruby
STYLE: Pitcher
HANDLE: Pulled back
COMPANY: Hamon
DATE: Late 1940s – 1970s
VALUE: $35.00 – $40.00

PLATE 97
HEIGHT: 4¼"
COLOR: Blue
STYLE: Miniature Pitcher
HANDLE: Drop over
COMPANY: Unknown
DATE: Unknown
VALUE: $30.00 – $35.00

PLATE 98
HEIGHT: 5"
COLOR: Emerald Green
STYLE: Pitcher
HANDLE: Pulled Back
COMPANY: Unknown
DATE: Unknown
VALUE: $25.00 – $30.00

PLATE 99
HEIGHT: 5½"
COLOR: Light Amber
STYLE: Pitcher
HANDLE: Pulled back
COMPANY: Unknown
DATE: Unknown
VALUE: $25.00 – $30.00

PLATE 100
HEIGHT: 5"
COLOR: Topaz
STYLE: Pitcher
HANDLE: Pulled back
COMPANY: Unknown
DATE: Unknown
VALUE: $25.00 – $30.00

PLATE 101
HEIGHT: 4⅛"
COLOR: Olive Green
STYLE: Miniature Pitcher
HANDLE: Pulled back
COMPANY: Unknown
DATE: Unknown
VALUE: $15.00 – $20.00
REMARKS: This piece is badly made. The handle is crooked and it has air bubbles.

PLATE 102
HEIGHT: 5"
COLOR: Ruby
STYLE: Miniature Pitcher
HANDLE: Pulled back
COMPANY: Pilgrim
DATE: 1949 – 1969
VALUE: $30.00 – $35.00

PLATE 103
HEIGHT: 4¾"
COLOR: Tangerine
STYLE: Miniature Pitcher
HANDLE: Drop over
COMPANY: Pilgrim
DATE: 1949 – 1969
VALUE: $30.00 – $35.00

PLATE 104
HEIGHT: 4¾"
COLOR: Tangerine
STYLE: Miniature Pitcher
HANDLE: Pulled back
COMPANY: Pilgrim
DATE: 1949 – 1969
VALUE: $30.00 – $35.00

PLATE 105
HEIGHT: 4½"
COLOR: Amberina
STYLE: Miniature Pitcher
HANDLE: Drop over
COMPANY: Pilgrim
DATE: 1949 – 1969
VALUE: $30.00 – $35.00

PLATE 106
HEIGHT: 4¾"
COLOR: Tangerine
STYLE: Miniature Pitcher
HANDLE: Pulled back
COMPANY: Pilgrim
DATE: 1949 – 1969
VALUE: $30.00 – $35.00

PLATE 107
HEIGHT: 4½"
COLOR: Ruby
STYLE: Miniature Pitcher
HANDLE: Pulled back
COMPANY: Pilgrim
DATE: 1949 – 1969
VALUE: $30.00 – $35.00
REMARKS: Note how the neck
           slants to the right.

PLATE 108
HEIGHT: 4½"
COLOR: Ruby
STYLE: Miniature Pitcher
HANDLE: Pulled back
COMPANY: Pilgrim
DATE: 1949 – 1969
VALUE: $30.00 – $35.00

PLATE 109
HEIGHT: 4½"
COLOR: Blue
STYLE: Miniature Pitcher
HANDLE: Pulled back
COMPANY: Pilgrim
DATE: 1949 – 1969
VALUE: $25.00 – $30.00

PLATE 110
HEIGHT: 4½"
COLOR: Lemon Lime
STYLE: Miniature Pitcher
HANDLE: Pulled back
COMPANY: Pilgrim
DATE: 1949 – 1969
VALUE: $25.00 – $30.00

PLATE 111
HEIGHT: 4½"
COLOR: Topaz
STYLE: Miniature Pitcher
HANDLE: Ribbed, crystal drop over
COMPANY: Pilgrim
DATE: 1949 – 1969
VALUE: $35.00 – $40.00
REMARKS: Ribbed handle pieces are priced higher.

PLATE 112
HEIGHT: 4½"
COLOR: Topaz
STYLE: Miniature Pitcher
HANDLE: Drop over
COMPANY: Pilgrim
DATE: 1949 – 1969
VALUE: $25.00 – $30.00

PLATE 113
HEIGHT: 4¼"
COLOR: Light Orange
STYLE: Miniature Pitcher
HANDLE: Pulled back
COMPANY: Pilgrim
DATE: 1949 – 1969
VALUE: $25.00 – $30.00

PLATE 114
HEIGHT: 4¾"
COLOR: Amber
STYLE: Pitcher
HANDLE: Pulled back
COMPANY: Unknown
DATE: Unknown
VALUE: $45.00 – $50.00

PLATE 115
HEIGHT: 5½"
COLOR: Emerald Green
STYLE: Miniature Pitcher
HANDLE: Pulled back
COMPANY: Unknown
DATE: Unknown
VALUE: $45.00 – $50.00

PLATE 116
HEIGHT: 5½"
COLOR: Amberina
STYLE: Pitcher
HANDLE: Drop over (yellow)
COMPANY: Unknown
DATE: Unknown
VALUE: $50.00 – $55.00

PLATE 117
HEIGHT: 5½"
COLOR: Amberina
STYLE: Pitcher
HANDLE: Drop over (orange)
COMPANY: Unknown
DATE: Unknown
VALUE: $50.00 – $55.00

PLATE 118
HEIGHT: 3¼"
COLOR: Ruby
STYLE: Miniature Pitcher
HANDLE: Drop over
COMPANY: Kanawha
DATE: 1957 – 1987
VALUE: $30.00 – $35.00

PLATE 119
HEIGHT: 3¼"
COLOR: Amberina
STYLE: Miniature Pitcher
HANDLE: Drop over
COMPANY: Kanawha
DATE: 1957 – 1987
VALUE: $30.00 – $35.00

PLATE 120
HEIGHT: 3¾"
COLOR: Olive Green
STYLE: Pitcher
HANDLE: Pulled back
COMPANY: Rainbow
DATE: Late 1940s – 1960s
VALUE: $35.00 – $40.00

PLATE 121
HEIGHT: 3¾"
COLOR: Topaz
STYLE: Miniature Pitcher
HANDLE: Pulled back
COMPANY: Rainbow
DATE: Late 1940s – 1960s
VALUE: $35.00 – $40.00

PLATE 122
HEIGHT: 4¼"
COLOR: Blue
STYLE: Pitcher
HANDLE: Drop over
COMPANY: Rainbow
DATE: Late 1940s – 1960s
VALUE: $45.00 – $50.00

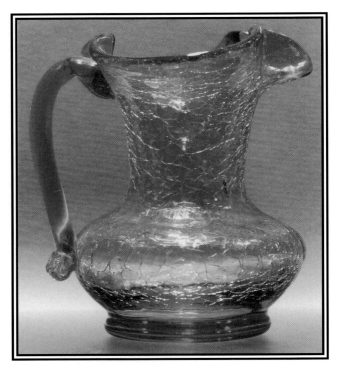

PLATE 124
HEIGHT: 4"
COLOR: Blue
STYLE: Miniature Pitcher
HANDLE: Pulled back
COMPANY: Kanawha
DATE: 1957 – 1987
VALUE: $25.00 – $30.00

PLATE 123
HEIGHT: 4"
COLOR: Blue
STYLE: Miniature Pitcher
HANDLE: Pulled back
COMPANY: Unknown
DATE: Unknown
VALUE: $25.00 – $30.00

PLATE 125
HEIGHT: 4⅛"
COLOR: Topaz
STYLE: Miniature Pitcher
HANDLE: Pulled back
COMPANY: Kanawha
DATE: 1957 – 1987
VALUE: $25.00 – $30.00

PLATE 126
HEIGHT: 4½"
COLOR: Amberina
STYLE: Pitcher
HANDLE: Drop over
COMPANY: Unknown
DATE: Unknown
VALUE: $50.00 – $55.00

PLATE 127
HEIGHT: 4½"
COLOR: Ruby
STYLE: Pitcher
HANDLE: Drop over
COMPANY: Unknown
DATE: Unknown
VALUE: $50.00 – $55.00

PLATE 128
HEIGHT: 4"
COLOR: Ruby
STYLE: Pitcher
HANDLE: Drop over
COMPANY: Rainbow
DATE: Late 1940s – 1960s
VALUE: $50.00 – $55.00

PLATE 130
HEIGHT: 4¾"
COLOR: Amberina
STYLE: Pitcher
HANDLE: Drop over
COMPANY: Rainbow
DATE: Late 1940s – 1960s
VALUE: $50.00 – $55.00

PLATE 129
HEIGHT: 4½"
COLOR: Turquoise
STYLE: Pitcher
HANDLE: Drop over
COMPANY: Rainbow
DATE: Late 1940s – 1960s
VALUE: $45.00 – $50.00

PLATE 131
HEIGHT: 4¾"
COLOR: Tangerine
STYLE: Pitcher
HANDLE: Drop over
COMPANY: Rainbow
DATE: Late 1940s – 1960s
VALUE: $50.00 – $55.00

PLATE 132
HEIGHT: 5¼"
COLOR: Amberina
STYLE: Pitcher
HANDLE: Pulled Back
COMPANY: Rainbow
DATE: Late 1940s – 1960s
VALUE: $50.00 – $55.00

PLATE 133
HEIGHT: 5"
COLOR: Amberina
STYLE: Pitcher
HANDLE: Pulled back
COMPANY: Rainbow
DATE: Late 1940s – 1960s
VALUE: $50.00 – $55.00

PLATE 134
HEIGHT: 3¾"
COLOR: Amberina
STYLE: Miniature Pitcher
HANDLE: Drop over
COMPANY: Unknown
DATE: Unknown
VALUE: $40.00 – $45.00

PLATE 135
HEIGHT: 3½"
COLOR: Emerald Green
STYLE: Miniature Pitcher
HANDLE: Pulled back
COMPANY: Kanawha
DATE: 1957 – 1987
VALUE: $30.00 – $35.00

PLATE 136
HEIGHT: 5½"
COLOR: Topaz
STYLE: Pitcher
HANDLE: Pulled back
COMPANY: Rainbow
DATE: Late 1940s – 1960s
VALUE: 50.00 – $55.00

Close-up of Plate 137.

PLATE 137
HEIGHT: 4¾"
COLOR: Green
STYLE: Pitcher
HANDLE: Pulled back
COMPANY: Williamsburg Glass Company
DATE: 1950 – 1960
VALUE: $55.00 – $60.00
REMARKS: Labels increase the price.

PLATE 138
HEIGHT: 4½"
COLOR: Green
STYLE: Pitcher
HANDLE: Pulled back
COMPANY: Rainbow
DATE: Late 1940s – 1960s
VALUE: $45.00 – $50.00
REMARKS: Courtesy of Bayvillage
                     Gardens & Antiques,
                     Amityville, Long Island.

PLATE 139
HEIGHT: 5"
COLOR: Emerald Green
STYLE: Pitcher
HANDLE: Drop over
COMPANY: Unknown
DATE: Unknown
VALUE: $45.00 – $50.00

PLATE 140
HEIGHT: 5"
COLOR: Cream
STYLE: Pitcher
HANDLE: Drop over
COMPANY: Unknown
DATE: Unknown
VALUE: $45.00 – $50.00

PLATE 141
HEIGHT: 4"
COLOR: Amberina
STYLE: Miniature Pitcher
HANDLE: Drop over
COMPANY: Rainbow
DATE: Late 1940s – 1960s
VALUE: $45.00 – $50.00

PLATE 142
HEIGHT: 3½"
COLOR: Topaz
STYLE: Miniature Pitcher
HANDLE: Drop over
COMPANY: Unknown
DATE: Unknown
VALUE: $20.00 – $25.00

PLATE 143
HEIGHT: 3¾"
COLOR: Topaz
STYLE: Miniature Pitcher
HANDLE: Drop over
COMPANY: Unknown
DATE: Unknown
VALUE: $20.00 – $25.00
REMARKS: Blown into a mold.

PLATE 144
HEIGHT: 4"
COLOR: Blue
STYLE: Miniature Pitcher
HANDLE: Pulled back
COMPANY: Kanawha
DATE: 1957 – 1987
VALUE: $25.00 – $30.00

PLATE 145
HEIGHT: 4¼"
COLOR: Light Amber
STYLE: Miniature Pitcher
HANDLE: Drop over
COMPANY: Pilgrim
DATE: 1949 – 1969
VALUE: $25.00 – $30.00

PLATE 146
HEIGHT: 4½"
COLOR: Amberina
STYLE: Miniature Pitcher
HANDLE: Pulled back
COMPANY: Hamon
DATE: Date 1940s – 1970s
VALUE: $30.00 – $35.00

PLATE 147
HEIGHT: 4¼"
COLOR: Dark Topaz
STYLE: Miniature Pitcher
HANDLE: Drop over
COMPANY: Pilgrim
DATE: 1949 – 1969
VALUE: $25.00 – $30.00

PLATE 148
HEIGHT: 3½"
COLOR: Olive Green
STYLE: Miniature Pitcher
HANDLE: Drop over
COMPANY: Pilgrim
DATE: 1949 – 1969
VALUE: $25.00 – $30.00

PLATE 149
HEIGHT: 5"
COLOR: Topaz
STYLE: Pitcher
HANDLE: Drop over
COMPANY: Pilgrim
DATE: 1949 – 1969
VALUE: $30.00 – $35.00

PLATE 150
HEIGHT: 5"
COLOR: Olive Green
STYLE: Pitcher
HANDLE: Pulled back
COMPANY: Unknown
DATE: Unknown
VALUE: $25.00 – $30.00
REMARKS: This is not a high quality
            piece. It has a crooked
            handle, very little crackle,
            and large air bubbles.

PLATE 151
HEIGHT: 5½"
COLOR: Green
STYLE: Pitcher
HANDLE: Drop over
COMPANY: Kanawha
DATE: 1957 – 1987
VALUE: $40.00 – $45.00

PLATE 152
HEIGHT: 5¼"
COLOR: Amberina
STYLE: Pitcher
HANDLE: Pulled back
COMPANY: Kanawha
DATE: 1957 – 1987
VALUE: $60.00 – $65.00
REMARKS: Labels increase the value.

PLATE 153
HEIGHT: 5¼"
COLOR: Green
STYLE: Pitcher
HANDLE: Drop over
COMPANY: Unknown
DATE: Unknown
VALUE: $25.00 – $30.00
REMARKS: Blown into a mold.

PLATE 154
HEIGHT: 5¼"
COLOR: Dark Blue
STYLE: Pitcher
HANDLE: Drop over
COMPANY: Unknown
DATE: Unknown
VALUE: $25.00 – $30.00
REMARKS: Blown into a mold.
           Courtesy of Bayvillage
           Gardens & Antiques,
           Amityville, Long Island.

PLATE 155
HEIGHT: 5¼"
COLOR: Emerald Green
STYLE: Pitcher
HANDLE: Drop over
COMPANY: Unknown
DATE: Unknown
VALUE: $25.00 – $30.00
REMARKS: Blown into a mold.

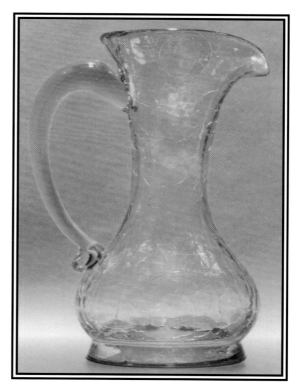

PLATE 156
HEIGHT: 5¼"
COLOR: Gold
STYLE: Pitcher
HANDLE: Pulled back
COMPANY: Kanawha
DATE: 1957 – 1987
VALUE: $40.00 – $45.00
REMARKS: Blown into a mold.

PLATE 157
HEIGHT: 5"
COLOR: Green
STYLE: Pitcher
HANDLE: Pulled back
COMPANY: Kanawha
DATE: 1957 – 1987
VALUE: $40.00 – $45.00
REMARKS: Blown into a mold.

PLATE 158
HEIGHT: 6¼"
COLOR: Green
STYLE: Pitcher
HANDLE: Pulled back
COMPANY: Kanawha
DATE: 1957 – 1987
VALUE: $40.00 – $45.00
REMARKS: Courtesy of Bayvillage
            Gardens & Antiques,
            Amityville, Long Island.

PLATE 159
HEIGHT: 6¼"
COLOR: Olive Green
STYLE: Pitcher
HANDLE: Drop over
COMPANY: Kanawha
DATE: 1957 – 1987
VALUE: $40.00 – $50.00

PLATE 160
HEIGHT: 4½"
COLOR: Charcoal
STYLE: Pitcher
HANDLE: Drop over
COMPANY: Unknown
DATE: Unknown
VALUE: $50.00 – $55.00
REMARKS: Rare color.

PLATE 161
HEIGHT: 4½"
COLOR: Topaz
STYLE: Pitcher
HANDLE: Pulled back
COMPANY: Unknown
DATE: Unknown
VALUE: $15.00 – $20.00
REMARKS: Only the bottom
            is crackled.

PLATE 162
HEIGHT: 5"
COLOR: Blue
STYLE: Pitcher
HANDLE: Drop over
COMPANY: Pilgrim
DATE: 1949 – 1969
VALUE: $40.00 – $45.00

PLATE 163
HEIGHT: 5¼"
COLOR: Ruby
STYLE: Pitcher
HANDLE: Pulled back
COMPANY: Unknown
DATE: Unknown
VALUE: $50.00 – $55.00

PLATE 164
HEIGHT: 4¾"
COLOR: Blue
STYLE: Pitcher
HANDLE: Pulled back
COMPANY: Unknown
DATE: Unknown
VALUE: $45.00 – $50.00

PLATE 165
HEIGHT: 3½"
COLOR: Amberina (Tangerine)
STYLE: Miniature Pitcher
HANDLE: Drop over
COMPANY: Probably Blenko
DATE: Unknown
VALUE: $30.00 – $35.00

PLATE 166
HEIGHT: 5¾"
COLOR: Olive Green
STYLE: Large Wide-Mouth Pitcher
HANDLE: Drop over
COMPANY: Blenko
DATE: 1960s
VALUE: $45.00 – $50.00
REMARKS: The mouth is 4¼" wide.

PLATE 167
HEIGHT: 5"
COLOR: Tangerine
STYLE: Pitcher
HANDLE: Drop over
COMPANY: Pilgrim
DATE: 1949 – 1969
VALUE: $50.00 – $55.00

PLATE 168
HEIGHT: 6"
COLOR: Topaz
STYLE: Pitcher
HANDLE: Drop over
COMPANY: Pilgrim
DATE: 1949 – 1969
VALUE: $50.00 – $55.00

PLATE 169
HEIGHT: 6"
COLOR: Amberina
STYLE: Pitcher
HANDLE: Drop over
COMPANY: Pilgrim
DATE: 1949 – 1969
VALUE: $55.00 – $60.00

PLATE 170
HEIGHT: 6"
COLOR: Ruby
STYLE: Pitcher
HANDLE: Pulled back
COMPANY: Pilgrim
DATE: 1949 – 1969
VALUE: $60.00 – $65.00

PLATE 171
HEIGHT: 5½"
COLOR: Blue
STYLE: Pitcher
HANDLE: Pulled back
COMPANY: Hamon
DATE: Late 1940s – 1970s
VALUE: $45.00 – $50.00

PLATE 172
HEIGHT: 6"
COLOR: Ruby
STYLE: Pitcher
HANDLE: Drop over
COMPANY: Pilgrim
DATE: 1949 – 1969
VALUE: $55.00 – $60.00

PLATE 173
HEIGHT: 6"
COLOR: Blue
STYLE: Pitcher
HANDLE: Pulled back
COMPANY: Unknown
DATE: Unknown
VALUE: $65.00 – $75.00

PLATE 174
HEIGHT: 6"
COLOR: Tangerine
STYLE: Pinched Pitcher
HANDLE: Drop over
COMPANY: Rainbow
DATE: Late 1940s – 1960s
VALUE: $65.00 – $70.00

Pitchers and Cruets

PLATE 175
HEIGHT: 6½"
COLOR: Amberina
STYLE: Pitcher
HANDLE: Pulled down
COMPANY: Hamon
DATE: Late 1940s – 1970s
VALUE: $75.00 – $85.00

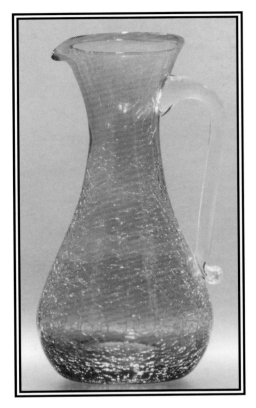

PLATE 176
HEIGHT: 7"
COLOR: Blue
STYLE: Pitcher
HANDLE: Pulled back
COMPANY: Pilgrim
DATE: 1940 – 1969
VALUE: $65.00 – $75.00

PLATE 177
HEIGHT: 8"
COLOR: Crystal with rose pink handle and rosette
STYLE: Pitcher
HANDLE: Drop over
COMPANY: Unknown
DATE: Unknown
VALUE: $100.00 – $124.00
REMARKS: Flashed handle and rosette.

Close-up of Plate 177.

PLATE 178
HEIGHT: 8"
COLOR: Topaz
STYLE: Pitcher
HANDLE: Amber pulled back
COMPANY: Rainbow
DATE: Late 1940s – 1960s
VALUE: $75.00 – $85.00
REMARKS: Courtesy of Bayville
            Gardens & Antiques,
            Amityville, Long Island.

PLATE 179
HEIGHT: 8¼"
COLOR: Amberina
STYLE: Pitcher
HANDLE: Drop over
COMPANY: Kanawha
DATE: 1957 – 1987
VALUE: $75.00 – $85.00

PLATE 180
HEIGHT: 8¼"
COLOR: Olive Green
STYLE: Pitcher
HANDLE: Pulled back
COMPANY: Probably Blenko
DATE: Unknown
VALUE: $85.00 – $100.00
REMARKS: Frilled top, 5¼" wide.

PLATE 181
HEIGHT: 8¼"
COLOR: Gold
STYLE: Pitcher
HANDLE: Drop over
COMPANY: Kanawha
DATE: 1957 – 1987
VALUE: $50.00 – $55.00

PLATE 182
HEIGHT: 8½"
COLOR: Topaz
STYLE: Pitcher
HANDLE: Drop over
COMPANY: Rainbow
DATE: Late 1940s – 1960s
VALUE: $50.00 – $75.00
REMARKS: Very fine cracks.

PLATE 183
HEIGHT: 9"
COLOR: Green
STYLE: Pitcher
HANDLE: Drop over (olive green)
COMPANY: Blenko
DATE: 1960s
VALUE: $75.00 – $85.00
REMARKS: Look at that handle!

PLATE 184
HEIGHT: 9¾"
COLOR: Wheat
STYLE: Pitcher
HANDLE: Drop over
COMPANY: Blenko
DATE: 1960s
VALUE: $60.00 – $75.00

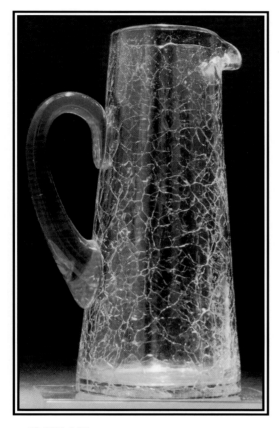

PLATE 185
HEIGHT: 10"
COLOR: Crystal with green handle
STYLE: Pitcher
HANDLE: Drop over
COMPANY: Unknown
DATE: Unknown
VALUE: $60.00 – $80.00

PLATE 186
HEIGHT: 10"
COLOR: Amberina
STYLE: Pitcher
HANDLE: Drop over
COMPANY: Unknown
DATE: Unknown
VALUE: $75.00 – $100.00

PLATE 187
HEIGHT: 10¼"
COLOR: Charcoal
STYLE: Pitcher
HANDLE: Drop over
COMPANY: Blenko
DATE: 1960s
VALUE: $75.00 – $100.00
REMARKS: Rare color.

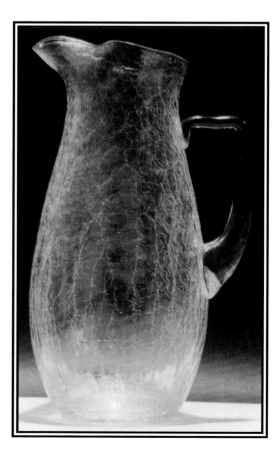

PLATE 188
HEIGHT: 10½"
COLOR: Smoke Gray
STYLE: Pitcher
HANDLE: Drop over
COMPANY: Unknown
DATE: Unknown
VALUE: $75.00 – $100.00

PLATE 189
HEIGHT: 12¼"
COLOR: Crystal
STYLE: Pitcher
HANDLE: Drop over
COMPANY: Unknown
DATE: Unknown
VALUE: $75.00 – $100.00

PLATE 190
HEIGHT: 12½"
COLOR: Crystal
STYLE: Pitcher
HANDLE: Drop over
COMPANY: Pilgrim
DATE: 1949 – 1969
VALUE: $75.00 – $100.00

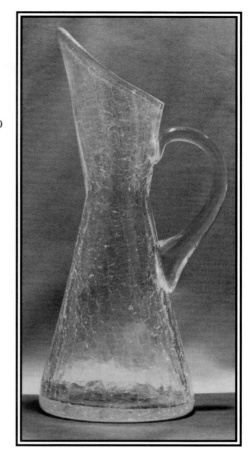

PLATE 191
HEIGHT: 12½"
COLOR: Sea Green
STYLE: Pitcher
HANDLE: Drop over
COMPANY: Blenko
DATE: 1950s
VALUE: $75.00 – $100.00

PLATE 192
HEIGHT: 13¼"
COLOR: Tangerine
STYLE: Pitcher
HANDLE: Drop over
COMPANY: Blenko
DATE: 1960s
VALUE: $100.00 – $125.00

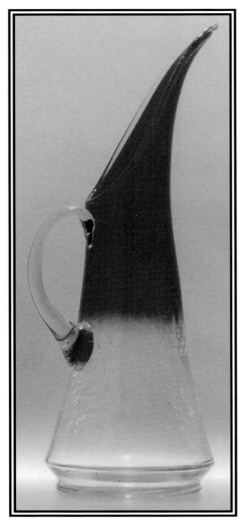

PLATE 193
HEIGHT: 13¼"
COLOR: Amberina
STYLE: Pitcher
HANDLE: Drop over
COMPANY: Kanawha
DATE: 1957 – 1987
VALUE: $75.00 – $85.00
REMARKS: Blown into a mold.

PLATE 194
HEIGHT: 17"
COLOR: Dark Amber
STYLE: Pitcher
HANDLE: Drop over
COMPANY: Blenko
DATE: 1949 – 1950
VALUE: $100.00 – $125.00
REMARKS: Hard to find this piece.

A cruet is a small stoppered glass bottle for vinegar, oil, and so on.

PLATE 195
HEIGHT: 4¼"
COLOR: Amber
STYLE: Cruets
HANDLE: Pulled back
COMPANY: Rainbow
DATE: Late 1940s – 1960s
VALUE: $70.00 – $80.00 (set)

PLATE 196
HEIGHT: 6"
COLOR: Sea Green
STYLE: Cruet
COMPANY: Pilgrim
DATE: 1949 – 1969
VALUE: $40.00 – $70.00

PLATE 197
HEIGHT: 6¼"
COLOR: Ruby
STYLE: Cruet
HANDLE: Pulled back
COMPANY: Rainbow
DATE: Late 1940s – 1960s
VALUE: $45.00 – $75.00

PLATE 198
HEIGHT: 6½"
COLOR: Blue
STYLE: Cruet
HANDLE: Pulled back
COMPANY: Rainbow
DATE: Late 1940s – 1960s
VALUE: $40.00 – $70.00

PLATE 199
HEIGHT: 6½"
COLOR: Amberina
STYLE: Cruet
HANDLE: Pulled back
COMPANY: Rainbow
DATE: Late 1940s – 1960s
VALUE: $45.00 – $75.00

PLATE 200
HEIGHT: 6½"
COLOR: Ruby
STYLE: Cruet
HANDLE: Pulled back
COMPANY: Pilgrim
DATE: 1949 – 1969
VALUE: $45.00 – $75.00

PLATE 201
HEIGHT: 7"
COLOR: Amberina
STYLE: Cruet
HANDLE: Pulled back
COMPANY: Rainbow
DATE: Late 1940s – 1960s
VALUE: $45.00 – $75.00

Vases

PLATE 202. A vase is a decorative container rounded and of greater height than width. It can be used as an ornament or for holding flowers.

PLATE 203
HEIGHT: 3½"
COLOR: Blue
STYLE: Vase
COMPANY: Pilgrim
DATE: 1949 – 1969
VALUE: $35.00 – $40.00

PLATE 204
HEIGHT: 4"
COLOR: Amethyst
STYLE: Minature Pinched Vase
COMPANY: Pilgrim
DATE: 1949 – 1969
VALUE: $60.00 – $80.00
REMARKS: Very fine cracks.
            Amethyst is a highly
            collectible color and
            warrants a higher price.

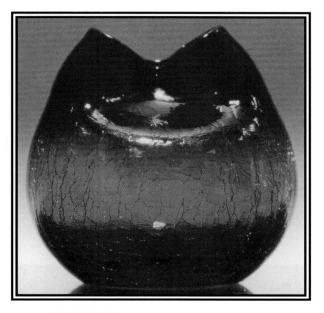

PLATE 205
HEIGHT: 4"
COLOR: Amberina
STYLE: Minature Pinched Vase
COMPANY: Pilgrim
DATE: 1949 – 1969
VALUE: $55.00 – $80.00
REMARKS: Very fine cracks.

PLATE 206
HEIGHT: 3¾"
COLOR: Sea Green
STYLE: Minature Pinched Vase
COMPANY: Blenko
DATE: Late 1940s – 1950s
VALUE: $50.00 – $75.00
REMARKS: Large cracks.

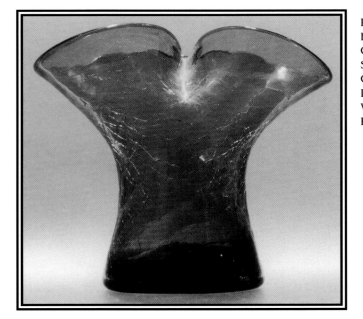

PLATE 207
HEIGHT: 4"
COLOR: Amethyst
STYLE: Double-neck Vase
COMPANY: Blenko
DATE: Late 1940s – 1950s
VALUE: $50.00 – $65.00
REMARKS: Amethyst is a highly
            collectible color and
            warrants a higher price.

PLATE 208
HEIGHT: 4"
COLOR: Olive Green
STYLE: Double-neck Vase
COMPANY: Blenko
DATE: Late 1940s – 1950s
VALUE: $50.00 – $75.00

PLATE 209
HEIGHT: 4"
COLOR: Emerald Green
STYLE: Double-neck Vase
COMPANY: Blenko
DATE: Late 1940s – 1950s
VALUE: $50.00 – $75.00

PLATE 210
HEIGHT: 4"
COLOR: Amethyst
STYLE: Minature Vase
COMPANY: Unknown
DATE: Unknown
VALUE: $50.00 – $75.00

PLATE 211
HEIGHT: 4¼"
COLOR: Sea Green
STYLE: Vase
COMPANY: Unknown
DATE: Unknown
VALUE: $30.00 – $35.00

PLATE 212
HEIGHT: 4½"
COLOR: Dark Amber
STYLE: Vase
COMPANY: Pilgrim
DATE: 1949 – 1969
VALUE: $50.00 – $55.00
REMARKS: Labels increase the price.

PLATE 213
HEIGHT: 4½"
COLOR: Blue
STYLE: Vase
COMPANY: Pilgrim
DATE: 1949 – 1969
VALUE: $40.00 – $45.00

PLATE 214
HEIGHT: 4½"
COLOR: Tangerine
STYLE: Minature Vase
COMPANY: Pilgrim
DATE: 1949 – 1969
VALUE: $50.00 – $75.00

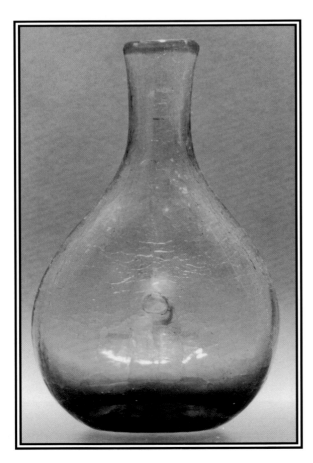

PLATE 215
HEIGHT: 5"
COLOR: Lemon Lime
STYLE: Pinched Vase
COMPANY: Pilgrim
DATE: 1949 – 1969
VALUE: $35.00 – $40.00
REMARKS: Strawberry pontil mark
               on bottom.

PLATE 216
HEIGHT: 5"
COLOR: Lemon Lime
STYLE: Minature Vase
COMPANY: Pilgrim
DATE: 1949 – 1969
VALUE: $45.00 – $65.00
REMARKS: Courtesy of Bayville
           Gardens & Antiques,
           Amityville, Long Island.

PLATE 217
HEIGHT: 5"
COLOR: Cranberry
STYLE: Vase
COMPANY: Unknown
DATE: Unknown
VALUE: $45.00 – $65.00
REMARKS: Flashed on Cranberry.
           If this was real cranberry
           glass the price would be
           much higher.

PLATE 218
HEIGHT: 5"
COLOR: Blue
STYLE: Vase
COMPANY: Pilgrim
DATE: 1949 – 1969
VALUE: $45.00 – $65.00

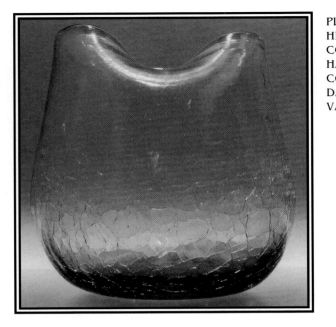

PLATE 219
HEIGHT: 5"
COLOR: Topaz
HANDLE: Pinched Vase
COMPANY: Unknown
DATE: Unknown
VALUE: $35.00 – $40.00

PLATE 220
HEIGHT: 5"
COLOR: Ruby
STYLE: Vase
COMPANY: Unknown
DATE: Unknown
VALUE: $65.00 – $75.00

PLATE 221
HEIGHT: 5½"
COLOR: Amberina
STYLE: Minature Vase
COMPANY: Unknown
DATE: Unknown
VALUE: $75.00 – $85.00

PLATE 222
HEIGHT: 5¼"
COLOR: Emerald Green
STYLE: Vase
COMPANY: Unknown
DATE: Unknown
VALUE: $25.00 – $30.00
REMARKS: Courtesy of Bayvillage
             Gardens & Antiques,
             Amityville, Long Island.

PLATE 223
HEIGHT: 5¼"
COLOR: Tangerine
STYLE: Vase
COMPANY: Rainbow
DATE: Late 1940s – 1960s
VALUE: $60.00 – $65.00

PLATE 225
HEIGHT: 5¼"
COLOR: Amberina with yellow top
STYLE: Vase
COMPANY: Unknown
DATE: Unknown
VALUE: $75.00 – $85.00

PLATE 224
HEIGHT: 5¼"
COLOR: Pale Sea Green
STYLE: Candleholder
COMPANY: Blenko
DATE: 1960s
VALUE: $50.00 – $65.00

PLATE 226
HEIGHT: 5¼"
COLOR: Ruby
STYLE: Vase
COMPANY: Rainbow
DATE: Late 1940s – 1970s
VALUE: $50.00 – $75.00

PLATE 227
HEIGHT: 5¼"
COLOR: Blue
STYLE: Minature Vase
COMPANY: Unknown
DATE: Unknown
VALUE: $30.00 – $40.00

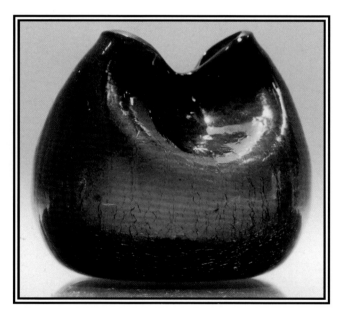

PLATE 228
HEIGHT: 5½"
COLOR: Emerald Green
STYLE: Pinched Vase
COMPANY: Pilgrim
DATE: 1949 – 1969
VALUE: $75.00 – $100.00

PLATE 229
HEIGHT: 5½"
COLOR: Amberina
STYLE: Vase
COMPANY: Kanawha
DATE: 1959 – 1987
VALUE: $50.00 – $55.00

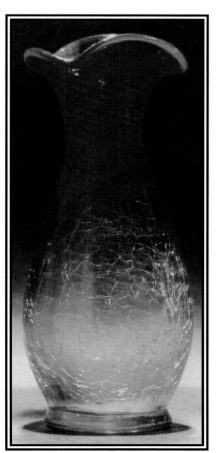

PLATE 230
HEIGHT: 5½"
COLOR: Smoke Gray
STYLE: Vase
COMPANY: Unknown
DATE: Unknown
VALUE: $60.00 – $65.00

PLATE 231
HEIGHT: 5½"
COLOR: Crystal
STYLE: Vase
COMPANY: Unknown
DATE: Unknown
VALUE: $40.00 – $50.00

PLATE 232
HEIGHT: 6½"
COLOR: Blue
STYLE: Vase
COMPANY: Pilgrim
DATE: 1949 – 1969
VALUE: $50.00 – $75.00

PLATE 233
HEIGHT: 7"
COLOR: Amberina (Blenko's tangerine)
STYLE: Vase
COMPANY: Blenko
DATE: 1961
VALUE: $75.00 – $85.00
REMARKS: Courtesy of Bayvillage
            Gardens & Antiques
            Amityville, Long Island.

PLATE 234
HEIGHT: 7"
COLOR: Crystal with blue rosettes
STYLE: Rosette Vase
COMPANY: Blenko
DATE: 1940s – 1950s
VALUE: $75.00 – $100.00

PLATE 235
HEIGHT: 7"
COLOR: Crystal with sea green leaves
STYLE: Leaf Beaker
COMPANY: Blenko
DATE: 1940s – 1950s
VALUE: $75.00 – $100.00

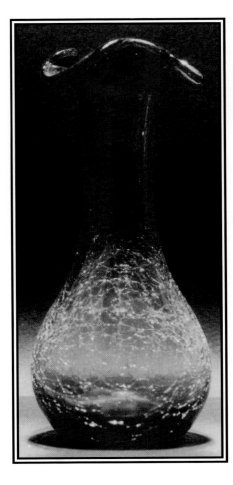

PLATE 236
HEIGHT: 7¼"
COLOR: Amberina
STYLE: Vase
COMPANY: Hamon
DATE: Late 1940s – 1970s
VALUE: $55.00 – $60.00

PLATE 237
HEIGHT: 7¼"
COLOR: Jonquil
STYLE: Footed Crimp Toe Vase
COMPANY: Blenko
DATE: 1950s
VALUE: $100.00 – $125.00
REMARKS: This style vase was introduced
            in 1938 in crystal with a blue
            trim on the crimped top. Note
            close-up picture of vase taken at
            the Blenko Museum.

388 - 1938
CRIMP TOP VASE

Close-up of Plate 237.

PLATE 238
HEIGHT: 8"
COLOR: Tangerine (amberina)
STYLE: Footed Crimp Top Vase
COMPANY: Blenko
DATE: 1950s
VALUE: $110.00 – $135.00

PLATE 239
HEIGHT: 7½"
COLOR: Sea Green
STYLE: Vase
COMPANY: Probably Blenko
DATE: Unknown
VALUE: $75.00 – $100.00
REMARKS: In the late 1930s through the early 1950s Blenko put rosettes on their pieces.

PLATE 240
HEIGHT: 7½"
COLOR: Sea Green
STYLE: Vase
HANDLE: Drop over
COMPANY: Blenko
DATE: 1940s – 1950s
VALUE: $75.00 – $85.00
REMARKS: Odd-shaped handles.

PLATE 241
HEIGHT: 7¾"
COLOR: Amberina
STYLE: Vase
COMPANY: Kanawha
DATE: 1957 – 1987
VALUE: $60.00 – $85.00
REMARKS: Labels increase the price.

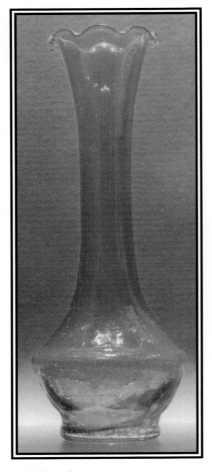

PLATE 243
HEIGHT: 8"
COLOR: Crystal
STYLE: Vase
COMPANY: Unknown
DATE: Unknown
VALUE: $35.00 – $40.00

PLATE 242
HEIGHT: 8"
COLOR: Orange
STYLE: Vase
COMPANY: Unknown
DATE: Unknown
VALUE: $40.00 – $45.00

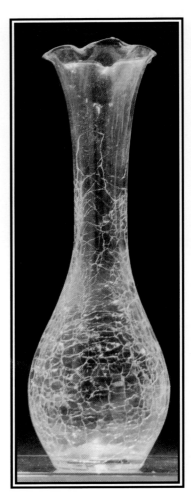

PLATE 244
HEIGHT: 8"
COLOR: Amberina
STYLE: Vase
COMPANY: Hamon
DATE: Late 1940s – 1970s
VALUE: $75.00 – $100.00

PLATE 245
HEIGHT: 8"
COLOR: Crystal with dark blue ears
STYLE: Ear Vase
COMPANY: Blenko
DATE: 1946
VALUE: $100.00 – $125.00

PLATE 246
HEIGHT: 8¼"
COLOR: Black Amethyst
STYLE: Vase
COMPANY: Unknown
DATE: Unknown
VALUE: $125.00 – $150.00
REMARKS: This color demands
            a very high price.

PLATE 247
HEIGHT: 8½"
COLOR: Crystal
STYLE: Fluted Vase
COMPANY: Blenko
DATE: 1940s – 1950s
VALUE: $75.00 – $100.00

PLATE 248
HEIGHT: 8¾"
COLOR: Crystal with blue rosettes
STYLE: Rose Urn
COMPANY: Blenko
DATE: 1940s – 1950s
VALUE: $90.00 – $110.00

PLATE 249
HEIGHT: 9¼"
COLOR: Olive Green
STYLE: Vase
COMPANY: Unknown
DATE: Unknown
VALUE: $50.00 – $60.00

PLATE 250
HEIGHT: 9½"
COLOR: Crystal with olive green leaves
STYLE: Leaf Beaker
COMPANY: Blenko
DATE: 1940s – 1950s
VALUE: $100.00 – $125.00

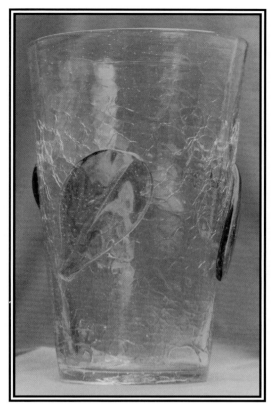

PLATE 251
HEIGHT: 9¾"
COLOR: Emerald Green
STYLE: Vase
COMPANY: Hamon
DATE: Late 1940s – 1970s
VALUE: $60.00 – $75.00

PLATE 252
HEIGHT: 10"
COLOR: Crystal
STYLE: Vase
COMPANY: Unknown
DATE: Unknown
VALUE: $75.00 – $100.00
REMARKS: Ribbed sides.

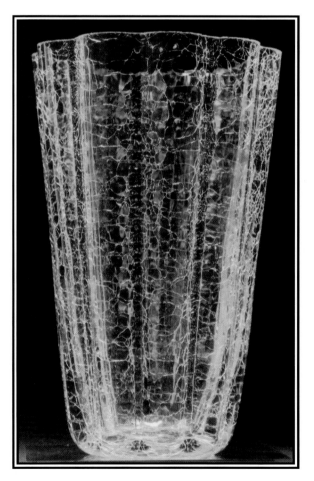

PLATE 253
HEIGHT: 10"
COLOR: Amberina
STYLE: Vase
COMPANY: Blenko
DATE: 1950s – 1960s
VALUE: $100.00 – $125.00

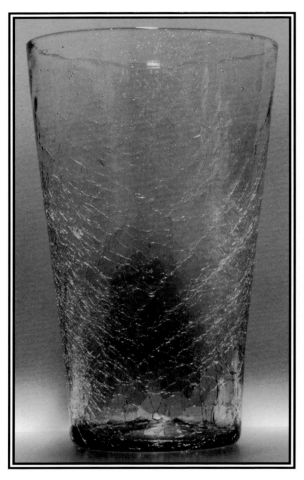

PLATE 254
HEIGHT: 10"
COLOR: Olive Green
STYLE: Vase
COMPANY: Blenko
DATE: Late 1940s – 1950s
VALUE: $75.00 – $100.00

PLATE 255
HEIGHT: 10½"
COLOR: Blue
STYLE: Vase
COMPANY: Bischoff
DATE: 1940 – 1963
VALUE: $100.00 – $125.00

PLATE 256
HEIGHT: 10¼"
COLOR: Topaz
STYLE: Vase
COMPANY: Probably Blenko
DATE: Unknown
VALUE: $100.00 – $125.00

PLATE 257
HEIGHT: 10¼"
COLOR: Amberina
STYLE: Vase
COMPANY: Unknown
DATE: Unknown
VALUE: $100.00 – $125.00

PLATE 258
HEIGHT: 11"
COLOR: Yellow (Jonquil)
STYLE: Fluted Vase
COMPANY: Blenko
DATE: 1940s – 1950s
VALUE: $100.00 – $125.00

PLATE 259
HEIGHT: 11¼"
COLOR: Smoke Gray
STYLE: Vase
COMPANY: Pilgrim
DATE: 1949 – 1969
VALUE: $100.00 – $125.00

PLATE 260
HEIGHT: 11¼"
COLOR: Olive Green
STYLE: Vase
COMPANY: Blenko
DATE: 1960s – 1970s
VALUE: $75.00 – $85.00

PLATE 261
HEIGHT: 11¼"
COLOR: Turquoise
STYLE: Vase
COMPANY: Blenko
DATE: 1960s – 1970s
VALUE: $75.00 – $85.00

PLATE 262
HEIGHT: 11½"
COLOR: Sea Green
STYLE: Vase
COMPANY: Blenko
DATE: 1960s
VALUE: $85.00 – $100.00

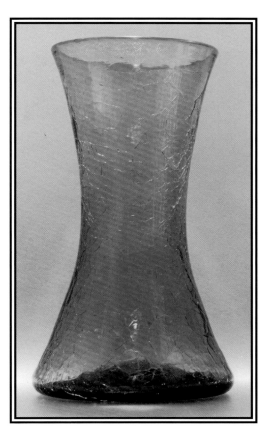

PLATE 263
HEIGHT: 11¾"
COLOR: Sea Green
STYLE: Vase
COMPANY: Blenko
DATE: 1950s
VALUE: $85.00 – $100.00

PLATE 264
HEIGHT: 12¼"
COLOR: Ruby
STYLE: Vase
COMPANY: Pilgrim
DATE: 1949 – 1969
VALUE: $125.00 – $150.00

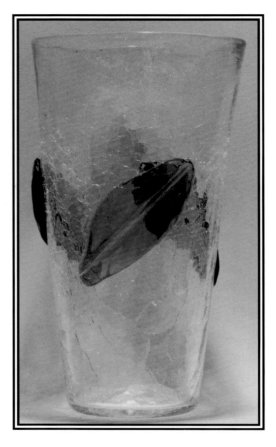

PLATE 265
HEIGHT: 13"
COLOR: Crystal with green leaves
STYLE: Leaf Beaker
COMPANY: Blenko
DATE: 1940s – 1950s
VALUE: $125.00 – $150.00

PLATE 266
HEIGHT: 17½"
COLOR: Gold
STYLE: Pinched Cylinder Vase
COMPANY: Blenko
DATE: Unknown
VALUE: $125.00 – $150.00

Decanters

PLATE 267. A decanter is a decorative stoppered bottle for serving wine, liquor, and so on.

PLATE 268
HEIGHT: 6"
COLOR: Lemon Lime
STYLE: Decanters
COMPANY: Pilgrim
DATE: 1949 – 1969
VALUE: $100.00 – $125.00 (for set)

PLATE 269
HEIGHT: 6¼"
COLOR: Topaz
STYLE: Decanters
HANDLE: Ribbed, crystal drop over
COMPANY: Pilgrim
DATE: 1949 – 1969
VALUE: $100.00 – $125.00 (for set)

PLATE 270
HEIGHT: 7¾"
COLOR: Ruby
STYLE: Decanters
COMPANY: Rainbow
DATE: Late 1940s – 1960s
VALUE: $125.00 – $150.00 (for set)

PLATE 271
HEIGHT: 7¾"
COLOR: Amberina
STYLE: Decanter
COMPANY: Rainbow
DATE: Late 1940s – 1960s
VALUE: $85.00 – $100.00
REMARKS: Crackled top.

PLATE 272
HEIGHT: 8¼"
COLOR: Amberina
STYLE: Decanters
COMPANY: Blenko
DATE: Early 1970s
VALUE: $150.00 – $175.00 (for set)

Close-up of Plate 272.

PLATE 273
HEIGHT: 8½"
COLOR: Topaz
STYLE: Decanter
COMPANY: Rainbow
DATE: Late 1940s – 1960s
VALUE: $75.00 – $100.00
REMARKS: Very fine cracks.

PLATE 274
HEIGHT: 9¼"
COLOR: Topaz
STYLE: Apothecary Jar
COMPANY: Probably Blenko
DATE: Unknown
VALUE: $75.00 – $85.00
REMARKS: Very large cracks.

PLATE 275
HEIGHT: 8"
COLOR: Topaz
STYLE: Decanter
COMPANY: Pilgrim
DATE: 1949 – 1969
VALUE: $60.00 – $75.00

PLATE 276
HEIGHT: 8¾"
COLOR: Topaz
STYLE: Decanter
COMPANY: Blenko
DATE: 1963
VALUE: $60.00 – $75.00

PLATE 277
HEIGHT: 10"
COLOR: Topaz
STYLE: Decanter
COMPANY: Rainbow
DATE: Late 1940s – 1960s
VALUE: $75.00 – $85.00

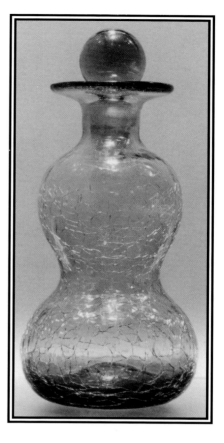

PLATE 278
HEIGHT: 10"
COLOR: Cobalt
STYLE: Pinched Decanter
COMPANY: Probably Blenko
DATE: Unknown
VALUE: $100.00 – $125.00
REMARKS: Cobalt demands higher prices.

PLATE 279
HEIGHT: 10½"
COLOR: Crystal with Olive Green top
STYLE: Decanter
COMPANY: Blenko
DATE: 1940s – 1950s
VALUE: $60.00 – $80.00

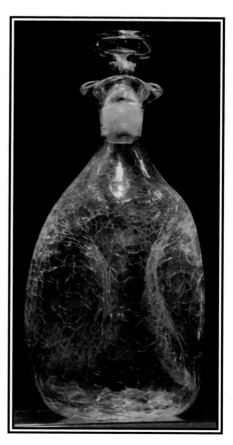

PLATE 280
HEIGHT: 13"
COLOR: Tangerine
COMPANY: Pilgrim
DATE: 1949 – 1969
VALUE: $75.00 – $100.00

PLATE 281
HEIGHT: 11¾"
COLOR: Charcoal (with blue tint)
STYLE: Decanter
COMPANY: Blenko
DATE: 1960s
VALUE: $75.00 – $100.00

PLATE 282
HEIGHT: 12"
COLOR: Sea Green
STYLE: Decanter
COMPANY: Pilgrim
DATE: 1949 – 1969
VALUE: $75.00 – $85.00
REMARKS: Note close-up picture of strawberry-looking mark found on the bottom of some of the Pilgrim pieces. Only Pilgrim used this technique of identification. Remember, not all Pilgrim pieces have this mark.

Close-up of Plate 282.

PLATE 283
HEIGHT: 12"
COLOR: Pale Amethyst (Lilac)
STYLE: Decanter
COMPANY: Pilgrim
DATE: 1949 – 1969
VALUE: $75.00 – $85.00

PLATE 284
HEIGHT: 12"
COLOR: Tangerine
STYLE: Decanter
COMPANY: Unknown
DATE: Unknown
VALUE: $75.00 – $100.00

PLATE 285
HEIGHT: 12½"
COLOR: Sea Green
STYLE: Decanter
COMPANY: Rainbow
DATE: Late 1940s – 1960s
VALUE: $100.00 – $125.00
REMARKS: Stopper is exquisitely
          made and is same length
          as the decanter body.

PLATE 286
HEIGHT: 12¾"
COLOR: Tangerine
STYLE: Decanter
COMPANY: Blenko
DATE: 1960s
VALUE: $75.00 – $100.00
REMARKS: Crackled top.

PLATE 287
HEIGHT: 13"
COLOR: Amberina
STYLE: Decanter
COMPANY: Blenko
DATE: 1960s
VALUE: $100.00 – $125.00
REMARKS: Crackled top.

PLATE 288
HEIGHT: 13¼"
COLOR: Topaz
STYLE: Decanter
COMPANY: Blenko
DATE: 1960s
VALUE: $75.00 – $100.00
REMARKS: Crackled top.

PLATE 289
HEIGHT: 13¼"
COLOR: Sea Green
STYLE: Decanter
COMPANY: Blenko
DATE: 1960s
VALUE: $75.00 – $100.00
REMARKS: Crackled top.

PLATE 290
HEIGHT: 14"
COLOR: Topaz
STYLE: Decanter
COMPANY: Rainbow
DATE: Late 1940s – 1960s
VALUE: $75.00 – $100.00
REMARKS: Crackled top.

PLATE 291
HEIGHT: 14½"
COLOR: Green
STYLE: Decanter
HANDLE: Royal Blue pulled back
COMPANY: Rainbow
DATE: Late 1940s – 1960s
VALUE: $100.00 – $125.00
REMARKS: The stopper is beautifully made.

PLATE 292
HEIGHT: 16½"
COLOR: Sea Green
STYLE: Decanter
COMPANY: Blenko
DATE: 1960s
VALUE: $100.00 – $125.00
REMARKS: Crackled top.

PLATE 293
HEIGHT: 17"
COLOR: Tangerine
STYLE: Decanter
COMPANY: Pilgrim
DATE: 1949 – 1969
VALUE: $100.00 – $125.00

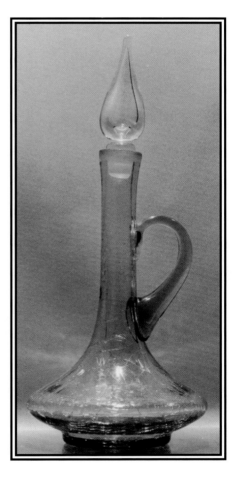

PLATE 294
HEIGHT: 17"
COLOR: Topaz
STYLE: Captain's Decanter
HANDLE: Drop over
COMPANY: Probably Blenko
DATE: Unknown
VALUE: $125.00 – $150.00

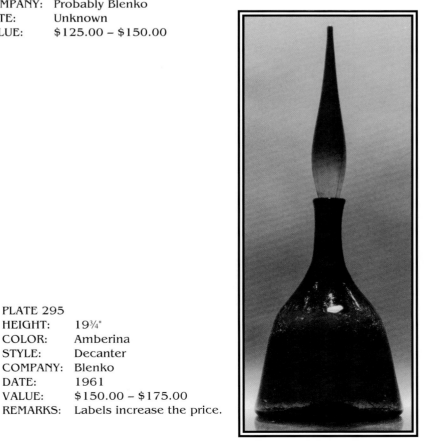

PLATE 295
HEIGHT: 19¾"
COLOR: Amberina
STYLE: Decanter
COMPANY: Blenko
DATE: 1961
VALUE: $150.00 – $175.00
REMARKS: Labels increase the price.

Jugs

PLATE 296. A jug is a pitcher with a narrow mouth and a handle used for holding liquids.

PLATE 297
HEIGHT: 4"
COLOR: Topaz
STYLE: Minature Jug
HANDLE: Crystal drop over
COMPANY: Pilgrim
DATE: 1949 – 1969
VALUE: $30.00 – $35.00

PLATE 298
HEIGHT: 4"
COLOR: Teal Green
STYLE: Minature Jug
HANDLE: Teal Green drop over
COMPANY: Pilgrim
DATE: 1949 – 1969
VALUE: $30.00 – $35.00

PLATE 299
HEIGHT: 4"
COLOR: Tangerine
STYLE: Minature Jug
HANDLE: Drop over
COMPANY: Pilgrim
DATE: 1949 – 1969
VALUE: $35.00 – $40.00

PLATE 300
HEIGHT: 4"
COLOR: Lemon Lime
STYLE: Minature Jug
HANDLE: Drop over
COMPANY: Pilgrim
DATE: 1949 – 1969
VALUE: $30.00 – $35.00

PLATE 301
HEIGHT: 4"
COLOR: Blue
STYLE: Minature Jug
HANDLE: Drop over
COMPANY: Pilgrim
DATE: 1949 – 1969
VALUE: $30.00 – $35.00

PLATE 302
HEIGHT: 6"
COLOR: Dark Blue
STYLE: Jug
HANDLE: Drop over
COMPANY: Unknown
DATE: Unknown
VALUE: $50.00 – $55.00
REMARKS: This piece has very fine cracks.

PLATE 303
HEIGHT: 6¾"
COLOR: Topaz
STYLE: Jug
HANDLE: Crystal drop over
COMPANY: Pilgrim
DATE: 1949 – 1969
VALUE: $65.00 – $70.00

PLATE 304
HEIGHT: 6¾"
COLOR: Dark Amber
STYLE: Jug
HANDLE: Drop over
COMPANY: Pilgrim
DATE: 1949 – 1969
VALUE: $55.00 – $60.00

PLATE 305
HEIGHT: 8¼"
COLOR: Amberina
STYLE: Jug
HANDLE: Gold drop over
COMPANY: Blenko
DATE: 1940s – 1950s
VALUE: $75.00 – $100.00

Cups, Glasses, and Mugs

PLATE 306. Cups, glasses, and mugs are different sized cylindrical drinking vessels.

PLATE 307
HEIGHT: 2¼"
COLOR: Amberina
STYLE: Cup
HANDLE: Drop over
COMPANY: Kanawha
DATE: 1957 – 1987
VALUE: $25.00 – $40.00

PLATE 308
HEIGHT: 2½"
COLOR: Light Sea Green
STYLE: Cup
HANDLE: Drop over
COMPANY: Unknown
DATE: Unknown
VALUE: $25.00 – $30.00

PLATE 309
HEIGHT: 4"
COLOR: Topaz
STYLE: Liqueur Glass
HANDLE: Drop over
COMPANY: Pilgrim
DATE: 1949 – 1969
VALUE: $40.00 – $45.00

PLATE 310
HEIGHT: 4"
COLOR: Blue
STYLE: Glass
HANDLE: Drop over
COMPANY: Pilgrim
DATE: 1949 – 1969
VALUE: $40.00 – $45.00

PLATE 311
HEIGHT: 5¾"
COLOR: Olive Green
STYLE: Wine Glass or Goblet
COMPANY: Unknown
DATE: Unknown
VALUE: $50.00 – $75.00
REMARKS: Rare.

PLATE 312
HEIGHT: 3½"
COLOR: Ruby
STYLE: Glass (tumbler)
COMPANY: Hamon
DATE: 1950s
VALUE: $40.00 – $60.00
REMARKS: This was a gift to us from Robert Hamon.

PLATE 313
HEIGHT: 6"
COLOR: Ruby
STYLE: Pinched Drinking Glass
COMPANY: Hamon
DATE: 1940s – 1970s
VALUE: $60.00 – $85.00

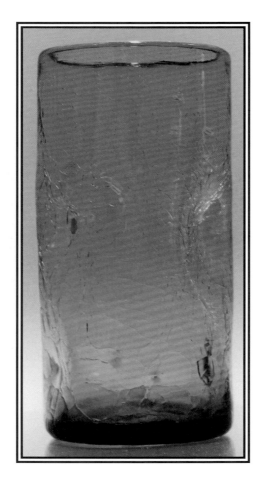

PLATE 314
HEIGHT: 5¾"
COLOR: Sea Green
STYLE: Glass
COMPANY: Blenko
DATE: Late 1940s – 1950s
VALUE: $50.00 – $75.00

PLATE 315
HEIGHT: 5¼"
COLOR: Emerald Green
STYLE: Glass
HANDLE: Drop over
COMPANY: Unknown
DATE: Unknown
VALUE: $35.00 – $50.00

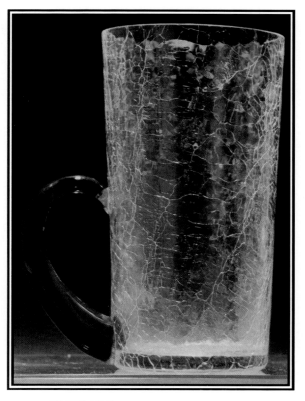

PLATE 316
HEIGHT: 5¼"
COLOR: Crystal
STYLE: Glass
HANDLE: Dark Amber drop over
COMPANY: Unknown
DATE: Unknown
VALUE: $35.00 – $50.00

PLATE 317
HEIGHT: 5½"
COLOR: Cream
STYLE: Glasses
HANDLE: Drop over
COMPANY: Unknown
DATE: Unknown
VALUE: $35.00 – $50.00 each

PLATE 318
HEIGHT: 6½"
COLOR: Crystal
STYLE: Glasses
COMPANY: Unknown
DATE: Unknown
VALUE: $35.00 – $50.00 each

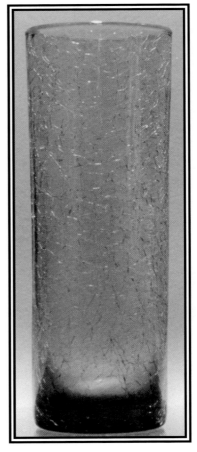

PLATE 319
HEIGHT: 6¾"
COLOR: Topaz
STYLE: Glass
COMPANY: Unknown
DATE: Unknown
VALUE: $35.00 – $50.00

PLATE 320
HEIGHT: 8"
COLOR: Crystal
STYLE: Glass
HANDLE: Drop over
COMPANY: Unknown
DATE: Unknown
VALUE: $40.00 – $45.00
REMARKS: Made in Czechoslovakia. This piece
            is labeled.

PLATE 321
HEIGHT: 6¼"
COLOR: Amber
STYLE: Mug
HANDLE: Drop over
COMPANY: Unknown
DATE: Late 1950s – early 1960s
VALUE: $25.00 – $30.00

PLATE 322
HEIGHT: 7¼"
COLOR: Emerald Green
STYLE: Large Glass
HANDLE: Drop over
COMPANY: Unknown
DATE: Unknown
VALUE: $50.00 – $75.00
REMARKS: Courtesy of Bayvillage Gardens & Antiques,
            Amityville, Long Island.

Fruit

PLATE 323. Crackle fruit is very hard to find since not very many pieces were made. We were told by Vivian Pridemore of Blenko Glass Company, that crackle fruit was never in their catalogs, and therefore, never a production item. For a store to purchase it, it had to place a special order.

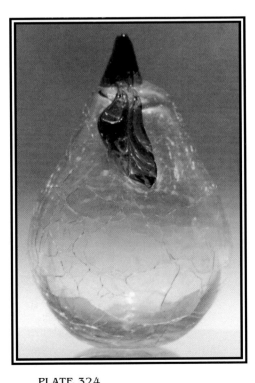

PLATE 324
HEIGHT: 5"
COLOR: Pale Sea Green
STYLE: Pear
COMPANY: Blenko
DATE: 1950s – 1960s
VALUE: $50.00 – $75.00

PLATE 325
HEIGHT: 4½"
COLOR: Cobalt
STYLE: Apple
COMPANY: Blenko
DATE: 1950s – 1960s
VALUE: $50.00 – $75.00

PLATE 326
HEIGHT: 3½"
COLOR: Ruby
STYLE: Apple
COMPANY: Blenko
DATE: 1950s – 1960s
VALUE: $50.00 – $75.00

PLATE 327
HEIGHT: 3¼"
COLOR: Emerald Green
STYLE: Apple
COMPANY: Hamon
DATE: Late 1940s – 1970s
VALUE: $50.00 – $75.00
REMARKS: Very fine cracks created using
            the sawdust technique.

PLATE 328
HEIGHT: 3¼"
COLOR: Crystal Pink
STYLE: Apple
COMPANY: Blenko
DATE: 1940s – 1950s
VALUE: $50.00 – $75.00

PLATE 329. In this section of potpourri, you will find a variety of unique pieces.

PLATE 330
HEIGHT: 7"
COLOR: Blue
STYLE: Perfume Bottle
COMPANY: Probably Italian made (Murano)
DATE: Unknown
VALUE: $75.00 – $100.00
REMARKS: Crystal top.

PLATE 331
HEIGHT: 5"
COLOR: Smoke Gray
STYLE: Perfume Bottle
COMPANY: Unknown
DATE: Unknown
VALUE: $75.00 – $100.00
REMARKS: Probably European.

PLATE 332
HEIGHT: 4½"
COLOR: Pale Blue
STYLE: Perfume Bottle
COMPANY: Unknown
DATE: Unknown
VALUE: $35.00 – $50.00
REMARKS: Probably European.

PLATE 333
HEIGHT: 4½"
COLOR: Light Blue
STYLE: Perfume Bottle
COMPANY: Unknown
DATE: Unknown
VALUE: $45.00 – $60.00
REMARKS: Probably European.

PLATE 334
HEIGHT: 3"
COLOR: Olive Green
STYLE: Perfume Bottle
COMPANY: Unknown
DATE: Unknown
VALUE: $25.00 – $30.00
REMARKS: Imported: I. Rice, New York
           imprinted on bottom of bottle.

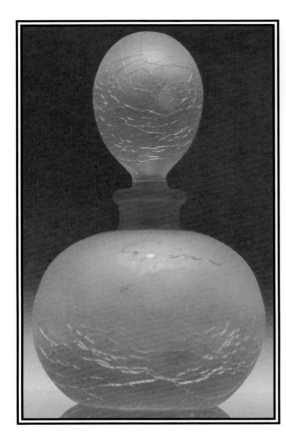

PLATE 335
HEIGHT: 4½"
COLOR: Pink
STYLE: Perfume Bottle
COMPANY: Unknown
DATE: 1980s
VALUE: $75.00 – $100.00
REMARKS: Signed Ivana (Trump). We were told by a
          reliable source that the manufacturer,
          who created this perfume bottle, did so
          without the consent of Ivana Trump.

PLATE 336
HEIGHT: 3¼"
COLOR: Amethyst
STYLE: Salt and Pepper Shakers
COMPANY: Unknown
DATE: Unknown
VALUE: $50.00 – $75.00 (for set)
REMARKS: Amethyst is highly collectible
          and warrants a higher price.

PLATE 337
HEIGHT: 4"
COLOR: Crystal
STYLE: Salt and Pepper Shakers
COMPANY: Unknown
DATE: Unknown
VALUE: $30.00 – $50.00 (for set)

PLATE 338
HEIGHT: 3½"
COLOR: Gold
STYLE: Sugar and Creamer
HANDLE: Gold drop over
COMPANY: Kanawha
DATE: 1957 – 1987
VALUE: $50.00 – $75.00 (for set)
REMARKS: Smooth bottom.

PLATE 339
HEIGHT: 3½"
COLOR: Blue
STYLE: Sugar and Creamer
HANDLE: Drop over
COMPANY: Pilgrim
DATE: 1949 – 1969
VALUE: $50.00 – $75.00 (for set)

PLATE 340
HEIGHT: 3⅛"
COLOR: Blue
STYLE: Creamer
HANDLE: Drop over
COMPANY: Unknown
DATE: Unknown
VALUE: $30.00 – $35.00

PLATE 341
HEIGHT: 3¾"
COLOR: Emerald Green
STYLE: Creamer
HANDLE: Drop over
COMPANY: Pilgrim
DATE: 1949 – 1969
VALUE: $30.00 – $35.00
REMARKS: Odd shaped handle.

PLATE 342
HEIGHT: 9"
COLOR: Topaz
STYLE: Fish Vase
COMPANY: Hamon
DATE: Late 1940s – 1970s
VALUE: $75.00 – $85.00
REMARKS: Rare.

PLATE 343
WIDTH: 16½" x 8¼" high
COLOR: Green
STYLE: Fish Vase
COMPANY: Hamon
DATE: Late 1940s – 1970s
VALUE: $100.00 – $125.00
REMARKS: Rare.

PLATE 344
HEIGHT: 15"
COLOR: Topaz
STYLE: Fish (wine bottle)
COMPANY: Unknown
DATE: Unknown
VALUE: $75.00 – $100.00
REMARKS: Green eyes.

PLATE 345
HEIGHT: 16"
COLOR: Topaz
STYLE: Fish (wine bottle)
COMPANY: Unknown
DATE: Unknown
VALUE: $125.00 – $150.00
REMARKS: Light green eyes. Import label dated
             1967. Labels increase the price.

PLATE 346
WIDTH: 21" x 9" high
COLOR: Topaz
STYLE: Fish (wine bottle)
COMPANY: Unknown
DATE: Unknown
VALUE: $135.00 – $160.00
REMARKS: Green eyes.

PLATE 347
HEIGHT: 2"
COLOR: Amberina
STYLE: Minature Hat
COMPANY: Kanawha
DATE: 1957 – 1987
VALUE: $35.00 – $40.00
REMARKS: Smooth bottom.

PLATE 348
HEIGHT: 2¾"
COLOR: Topaz
STYLE: Minature Hat
COMPANY: Blenko
DATE: 1940s – 1950s
VALUE: $35.00 – $40.00

PLATE 349
HEIGHT: 3"
COLOR: Olive Green
STYLE: Hat
COMPANY: Pilgrim
DATE: 1949 – 1969
VALUE: $35.00 – $40.00

PLATE 350
HEIGHT: 3"
COLOR: Topaz
STYLE: Hat
COMPANY: Pilgrim
DATE: 1949 – 1969
VALUE: $35.00 – $40.00

PLATE 352
WIDTH: 7¼"
COLOR: Amberina
STYLE: Ashtray
COMPANY: Unknown
DATE: Unknown
VALUE: $35.00 – $40.00

PLATE 351
HEIGHT: 5"
COLOR: Blue
STYLE: Hat
COMPANY: Pilgrim
DATE: 1949 – 1969
VALUE: $40.00 – $45.00
REMARKS: Small, fine cracks.

PLATE 353
WIDTH: 7¼"
COLOR: Dark Blue
STYLE: Ashtray
COMPANY: Unknown
DATE: Unknown
VALUE: $30.00 – $35.00
REMARKS: Courtesy of Bayvillage
                Gardens & Antiques,
                Amityville, Long Island.

PLATE 354
WIDTH: 7¾" x 3¾" high
COLOR: Dark Topaz
STYLE: Ashtray
COMPANY: Unknown
DATE: 1950s – 1960s
VALUE: $30.00 – $35.00

PLATE 355
HEIGHT: 3"
COLOR: Amberina
STYLE: Candy Dish
COMPANY: Kanawha
DATE: 1957 – 1987
VALUE: $40.00 – $45.00

PLATE 356
HEIGHT: 3"
COLOR: Gold
STYLE: Dish
COMPANY: Kanawha
DATE: 1957 – 1987
VALUE: $35.00 – $40.00

PLATE 357
WIDTH: 5¼" x 3"
COLOR: Green
STYLE: Dish
COMPANY: Kanawha
DATE: 1957 – 1987
VALUE: $35.00 – 40.00
REMARKS: Courtesy of Bayvillage
Gardens & Antiques,
Amityville, Long Island.

PLATE 358
WIDTH: 8" x 5" high
COLOR: Topaz
STYLE: Candy Bowl
COMPANY: Probably Blenko
DATE: Unknown
VALUE: $50.00 – $75.00

PLATE 359
WIDTH: 9" x 4"
COLOR: Crystal with green tint
STYLE: Candy Dish
COMPANY: Unknown
DATE: Unknown
VALUE: $50.00 – $75.00

PLATE 360
HEIGHT: 11¼", 7¾", 6"
COLOR: Yellow/Green
STYLE: Canister Set
COMPANY: Unknown
DATE: Unknown
VALUE: $250.00 – $300.00 (for set)
REMARKS: Rare. Vaseline (uranium)
            glass. Fluoresces under
            black light.

PLATE 361
HEIGHT: 5½"
COLOR: Tangerine
STYLE: Candy dish
COMPANY: Pilgrim
DATE: 1949 – 1969
VALUE: $100.00 – $125.00

PLATE 362
HEIGHT: 6"
COLOR: Amethyst
STYLE: Syrup Pitchers
HANDLE: Pulled back
COMPANY: Kanawha
DATE: 1957 – 1987
VALUE: $60.00 each
REMARKS: Amethyst is highly collectible and
            warrants a higher price.

PLATE 363
HEIGHT: 6"
COLOR: Blue
STYLE: Syrup Pitchers
HANDLE: Pulled back
COMPANY: Kanawha
DATE: 1957 – 1987
VALUE: $50.00 each
REMARKS: Labels increase the price.

Rare Finds

PLATE 364. Some of our pieces are very rare. We therefore felt it necessary to devote a special section for these unique pieces. The prices indicated are a reflection of their rarity.

PLATE 365
HEIGHT: 10¾"
COLOR: Crystal
STYLE: Decanter with glasses
HANDLE: Coral, drop over (glossy finish)
COMPANY: Unknown. Country: France.
DATE: Early 1900s
VALUE: Decanter: $200.00. Each glass: $50.00
REMARKS: Small glass – 2"; Large glass – 4".
Each piece is acid etched FRANCE on the bottom.

Close-up of Plate 366.

PLATE 366
HEIGHT: 8¾"
COLOR: Topaz
STYLE: Liquor Bottle
COMPANY: Unknown
DATE: Unknown
VALUE: Too rare to be priced
REMARKS: Scene applied after piece was
           crackled. May be European.

PLATE 367
HEIGHT: 10½"
COLOR: Crystal
STYLE: Decanter
COMPANY: Unknown
DATE: Unknown
VALUE: $150.00 – $200.00
REMARKS: Made in Czechoslovakia.

Close-up of Plate 367.

PLATE 368
HEIGHT: 10"
COLOR: Crystal
STYLE: Decanter
COMPANY: Unknown
DATE: Unknown
VALUE: $150.00 – $200.00
REMARKS: Made in Czechoslovakia.

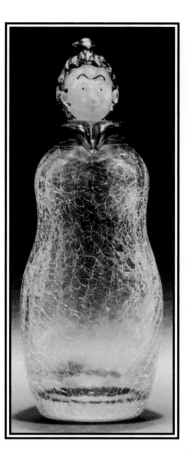

PLATE 369
HEIGHT: 6¾"
COLOR: Crystal
STYLE: Vase
COMPANY: Unknown
DATE: Unknown
VALUE: $100.00 – $125.00
REMARKS: Probably European.
Sterling silver top.

PLATE 370
HEIGHT: 9½"
COLOR: Amber
STYLE: Decanter
COMPANY: Most likely European
DATE: Unknown
VALUE: $150.00 – $200.00
REMARKS: Gold overlay on base, neck, and stopper. Very fine cracks.

PLATE 371
WIDTH: 5½" x 2¼"
COLOR: Dark Topaz
STYLE: Candy Dish
HANDLE: Ribbed drop over
COMPANY: Hamon
DATE: Late 1940s – 1970s
VALUE: $75.00 – $100.00

PLATE 372
HEIGHT: 8½"
COLOR: Amber
STYLE: Pitcher
HANDLE: Drop over
COMPANY: Unknown
DATE: Unknown
VALUE: $100.00 – $150.00
REMARKS: Probably European. Very fine
             cracks. Odd shaped handle.

PLATE 373
HEIGHT: 11½"
COLOR: Amber with Crystal foot
STYLE: Vase
COMPANY: Unknown
DATE: 1920s
VALUE: $125.00 – $150.00
REMARKS: Probably European.

PLATE 374
HEIGHT: 13½"
COLOR: Chartreuse
STYLE: Vase
COMPANY: Unknown
DATE: 1920s
VALUE: $150.00 – $200.00
REMARKS: Probably European.

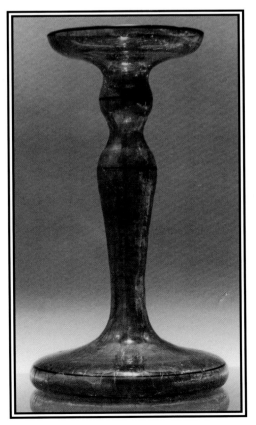

PLATE 375
HEIGHT: Pitcher, 7"; Glass, 4"
COLOR: Amber
STYLE: Pitcher and Glass
COMPANY: Unknown
DATE: Unknown
VALUE: $75.00 – $100.00

PLATE 376
HEIGHT: 10½"
COLOR: Apricot
STYLE: Candlestick Holder
COMPANY: Unknown
DATE: Unknown
VALUE: $50.00 – $75.00
REMARKS: Looks like carnival glass.
            Color flashed on.

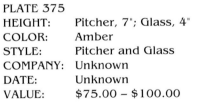

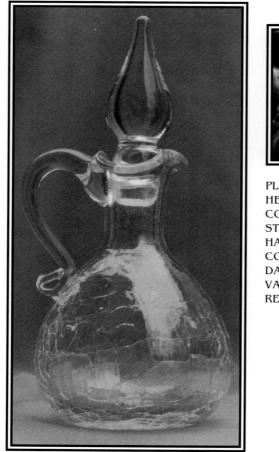

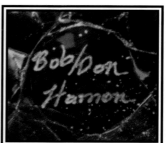

PLATE 377
HEIGHT: 9"
COLOR: Crystal
STYLE: Cruet
HANDLE: Pulled back
COMPANY: Hamon
DATE: December, 1994
VALUE: Priceless
REMARKS: This was a gift to us from
            Robert and Donald Hamon.

PLATE 378
HEIGHT: 4"
COLOR: Blue
STYLE: Cigarette Holder and Ashtray
COMPANY: Vogleson
DATE: 1949 – 1951
VALUE: Priceless
REMARKS: Too rare to be priced. Gift to
            us from Robert McKeand.

PLATES 379 & 380
HEIGHT: Cups, 2"; Ladle, 15" long
COLOR: Crystal with Amethyst handle
STYLE: Cups and Ladle
HANDLE: Hook
COMPANY: Blenko
DATE: 1950s
VALUE: Cups, $40.00 – $50.00 each;
            Ladle, $150.00 – $200.00

PLATE 381
WIDTH: 11¾" x 7" wide
COLOR: Crystal
STYLE: Punch Bowl
COMPANY: Blenko
DATE: 1950s
VALUE: $200.00 – $250.00

Bibliography

BOOKS

Eige, Eason and Rick Wilson. *Blenko Glass 1930–1953.* Marietta, Ohio: Antique Publications, 1987.

Ezell, Elaine and George Newhouse. *Cruets, Cruets, Cruets, Volume 1.* Marietta, Ohio: Antique Publications, 1991.

ARTICLES

Grayson, June. "Crackle Glass," *Glass Collector's Digest,* October/November 1989, Pgs. 50–54.

McKeand, Robert G. "A Brief History of the Pilgrim Glass Corporation," *The American Flint,* April 1993, pgs. 6 & 7.

BROCHURES & CATALOGS

Blenko Catalogs from 1940–1970. Courtesy of Blenko Glass Company.

Blenko Glass Booklet.

Hamon Glass Booklet.

Pilgrim Glass Corporation Catalog from 1949–1969. Courtesy of Robert McKeand.

Asheford Institute of Antiques Home Study Course – Volume 3.

About the Authors

Arlene and Stan Weitman are avid collectors of crackle glass. They also collect antiques and other collectibles. One of their serious hobbies is photography. The photographs in this book were done by them. They also stay fit by working out five or six days a week.

Arlene has a Master of Arts degree in education. She has been teaching elementary school in Valley Stream, Long Island, New York, for the past ten years. Recently, she has become a consultant for the U.C.S.M.P. Everyday Learning Corporation.

Stan has been a court reporter for the State of New York Workers' Compensation Board in Hempstead, Long Island, New York, for the past twenty-five years. He has taken an extensive course on antiques and is a certified appraiser.

If you have any questions relating to crackle glass, feel free to contact us at:

Stan Weitman
P.O. Box 1186
N. Massapequa, New York 11758
FAX (516)797-3039

❧ Books on Glass and Pottery ❧

This is only a partial listing of the books on antiques that are available from Collector Books. All books are well illustrated and contain current values. Most of the following books are available from your local bookseller, antique dealer, or public library. If you are unable to locate certain titles in your area, you may order by mail from COLLECTOR BOOKS, P.O. Box 3009, Paducah, KY 42002-3009. Customers with Visa or MasterCard may phone in orders from 7:00–4:00 CST, Monday–Friday, Toll Free 1-800-626-5420. Add $2.00 for postage for the first book ordered and $0.30 for each additional book. Include item number, title, and price when ordering. Allow 14 to 21 days for delivery.

GLASSWARE

1006	**Cambridge Glass** Reprint 1930–1934	$14.95
1007	**Cambridge Glass** Reprint 1949–1953	$14.95
2310	**Children's Glass Dishes, China & Furniture**, Vol. I, Lechler	$19.95
1627	**Children's Glass Dishes, China & Furniture**, Vol. II, Lechler	$19.95
3719	Coll. **Glassware from the 40's, 50's & 60's**, 2nd Ed., Florence	$19.95
2352	Collector's Encyclopedia of **Akro Agate Glassware**, Florence	$14.95
1810	Collector's Encyclopedia of **American Art Glass**, Shuman	$29.95
3312	Collector's Encyclopedia of **Children's Dishes**, Whitmyer	$19.95
3724	Collector's Encyclopedia of **Depression Glass**, 11th Ed., Florence	$19.95
1664	Collector's Encyclopedia of **Heisey Glass**, 1925–1938, Bredehoft	$24.95
3905	Collector's Encyclopedia of **Milk Glass**, Newbound	$24.95
1523	Colors In **Cambridge Glass**, National Cambridge Soceity	$19.95
1843	Covered **Animal Dishes**, Grist	$14.95
2275	**Czechoslovakian Glass** and Collectibles, Barta	$16.95
3882	**Elegant Glassware** of the Depression Era, 6th Ed., Florence	$19.95
1380	Encylopedia of **Pattern Glass**, McClain	$12.95
3981	Ever's Standard **Cut Glass** Value Guide	$12.95
3725	**Fostoria**, Pressed, Blown & Hand Molded Shapes, Kerr	$24.95
3883	**Fostoria Stemware**, The Crystal for America, Long & Seate	$24.95
3318	**Glass Animals** of the Depression Era, Garmon & Spencer	$19.95
1008	**Imperial Glass** Reprint 1904–1938, Archer	$14.95
3886	**Kitchen Glassware** of the Depression Years, 5th Ed., Florence	$19.95
2394	**Oil Lamps II**, Glass Kerosene Lamps	$24.95
3889	Pocket Guide to **Depression Glass**, 9th Ed., Florence	$9.95
3739	Standard Encylopedia of **Carnival Glass**, 4th Ed., Edwards	$24.95
3740	Standard **Carnival Glass** Price Guide, 9th Ed.	$9.95
3974	Standard Encylopedia of **Opalescent Glass**, Edwards	$19.95
1848	**Very Rare Glassware** of the Depression Years, Florence	$24.95
2140	**Very Rare Glassware** of the Depression Years, 2nd Series, Florence	$24.95
3326	**Very Rare Glassware** of the Depression Years, 3rd Series, Florence	$24.95
3909	**Very Rare Glassware** of the Depression Years, 4th Series, Florence	$24.95
2224	World of **Salt Shakers**, 2nd Ed., Lechner	$24.95

POTTERY

1312	**Blue & White Stoneware**, McNerney	$9.95
1958	So. Potteries **Blue Ridge Dinnerware**, 3rd Ed., Newbound	$14.95
1959	**Blue Willow**, 2nd Ed., Gaston	$14.95
3816	Collectible **Vernon Kilns**, Nelson	$24.95
3311	Collecting **Yellow Ware** – Id. & Value Guide, McAllister	$16.95
1373	Collector's Encyclopedia of **American Dinnerware**, Cunningham	$24.95
3815	Collector's Encyclopedia of **Blue Ridge Dinnerware**, Newbound	$19.95
2272	Collector's Encyclopedia of **California Pottery**, Chipman	$24.95
3811	Collector's Encyclopedia of **Colorado Pottery**, Carlton	$24.95
2133	Collector's Encyclopedia of **Cookie Jars**, Roerig	$24.95
3723	Collector's Encyclopedia of **Cookie Jars**, Volume II, Roerig	$24.95
3429	Collector's Encyclopedia of **Cowan Pottery**, Saloff	$24.95
2209	Collector's Encyclopedia of **Fiesta**, 7th Ed., Huxford	$19.95
3961	Collector's Encyclopedia of **Early Noritake**, Alden	$24.95
1439	Collector's Encyclopedia of **Flow Blue China**, Gaston	$19.95
3812	Collector's Encyclopedia of **Flow Blue China**, 2nd Ed., Gaston	$24.95

1813	Collector's Encyclopedia of **Geisha Girl Porcelain**, Litts	$19.95
3813	Collector's Encyclopedia of **Hall China**, 2nd Ed., Whitmyer	$24.95
3431	Collector's Encyclopedia of **Homer Laughlin China**, Jasper	$24.95
1276	Collector's Encyclopedia of **Hull Pottery**, Roberts	$19.95
3962	Collector's Encyclopedia of **Lefton China**, DeLozier	$19.95
2210	Collector's Encyclopedia of **Limoges Porcelain**, 2nd Ed., Gaston	$24.95
2334	Collector's Encyclopedia of **Majolica Pottery**, Katz-Marks	$19.95
1358	Collector's Encyclopedia of **McCoy Pottery**, Huxford	$19.95
3963	Collector's Encyclopedia of Metlox Potteries, Gibbs Jr.	$24.95
3313	Collector's Encyclopedia of **Niloak**, Gifford	$19.95
3837	Collector's Encyclopedia of **Nippon Porcelain I**, Van Patten	$24.95
2089	Collector's Ency. of **Nippon Porcelain**, 2nd Series, Van Patten	$24.95
1665	Collector's Ency. of **Nippon Porcelain**, 3rd Series, Van Patten	$24.95
3836	**Nippon Porcelain** Price Guide, Van Patten	$9.95
1447	Collector's Encyclopedia of **Noritake**, Van Patten	$19.95
3432	Collector's Encyclopedia of **Noritake**, 2nd Series, Van Patten	$24.95
1037	Collector's Encyclopedia of **Occupied Japan**, Vol. I, Florence	$14.95
1038	Collector's Encyclopedia of **Occupied Japan**, Vol. II, Florence	$14.95
2088	Collector's Encyclopedia of **Occupied Japan**, Vol. III, Florence	$14.95
2019	Collector's Encyclopedia of **Occupied Japan**, Vol. IV, Florence	$14.95
2335	Collector's Encyclopedia of **Occupied Japan**, Vol. V, Florence	$14.95
3964	Collector's Encyclopedia of **Pickard China**, Reed	$24.95
1311	Collector's Encyclopedia of **R.S. Prussia**, 1st Series, Gaston	$24.95
1715	Collector's Encyclopedia of **R.S. Prussia**, 2nd Series, Gaston	$24.95
3726	Collector's Encyclopedia of **R.S. Prussia**, 3rd Series, Gaston	$24.95
3877	Collector's Encyclopedia of **R.S. Prussia**, 4th Series, Gaston	$24.95
1034	Collector's Encyclopedia of **Roseville Pottery**, Huxford	$19.95
1035	Collector's Encyclopedia of **Roseville Pottery**, 2nd Ed., Huxford	$19.95
3357	**Roseville** Price Guide No. 10	$9.95
2083	Collector's Encyclopedia of **Russel Wright** Designs, Kerr	$19.95
3965	Collector's Encyclopedia of **Sasha Brastoff**, Conti, Bethany & Seay	$24.95
3314	Collector's Encyclopedia of **Van Briggle** Art Pottery, Sasicki	$24.95
2111	Collector's Encyclopedia of **Weller Pottery**, Huxford	$29.95
3452	Coll. Guide to Country Stoneware & Pottery, Raycraft	$11.95
2077	Coll. Guide to **Country Stoneware & Pottery**, 2nd Series, Raycraft	$14.95
3433	Collector's Guide To **Harker Pottery** - U.S.A., Colbert	$17.95
3434	Coll. Guide to **Hull Pottery**, The Dinnerware Line, Gick-Burke	$16.95
3876	Collector's Guide to **Lu-Ray Pastels**, Meehan	$18.95
2339	Collector's Guide to **Shawnee Pottery**, Vanderbilt	$19.95
1425	**Cookie Jars**, Westfall	$9.95
3440	**Cookie Jars**, Book II, Westfall	$19.95
3435	Debolt's Dictionary of **American Pottery Marks**	$17.95
2076	Early **Roseville Pottery**, Huxford	$7.95
1917	**Head Vases**, Identification & Values, Cole	$14.95
2379	Lehner's Ency. of **U.S. Marks** on Pottery, Porcelain & China	$24.95
3825	**Puritan Pottery**, Morris	$24.95
1670	**Red Wing Collectibles**, DePasquale	$9.95
1440	**Red Wing Stoneware**, DePasquale	$9.95
2350	**Royal Copley**, Wolfe	$14.95
2351	More **Royal Copley**, Wolfe	$14.95
3738	**Shawnee Pottery**, Mangus	$24.95
3327	**Watt Pottery** – Identification & Value Guide, Morris	$19.95

BOOKS ON COLLECTIBLES

This is only a partial listing of the books on antiques that are available from Collector Books. All books are well illustrated and contain current values. Most of the following books are available from your local bookseller, antique dealer, or public library. If you are unable to locate certain titles in your area, you may order by mail from COLLECTOR BOOKS, P.O. Box 3009, Paducah, KY 42002-3009. Customers with Visa or MasterCard may phone in orders from 7:00–4:00 CST, Monday–Friday, Toll Free 1-800-626-5420. Add $2.00 for postage for the first book ordered and $0.30 for each additional book. Include item number, title, and price when ordering. Allow 14 to 21 days for delivery.

DOLLS, FIGURES & TEDDY BEARS

2382	**Advertising Dolls**, Identification & Values, Robison & Sellers	$9.95
2079	**Barbie** Doll Fashions, Volume I, Eames	$24.95
3957	**Barbie** Exclusives, Rana	$18.95
3310	**Black Dolls**, 1820–1991, Perkins	$17.95
3873	**Black Dolls**, Book II, Perkins	$17.95
3810	**Chatty Cathy** Dolls, Lewis	$15.95
2021	Collector's **Male Action Figures**, Manos	$14.95
1529	Collector's Encyclopedia of **Barbie** Dolls, DeWein	$19.95
3727	Collector's Guide to **Ideal Dolls**, Izen	$18.95
3728	Collector's Guide to Miniature **Teddy Bears**, Powell	$17.95
4506	**Dolls in Uniform**, Bourgeois	$18.95
3967	Collector's Guide to **Trolls**, Peterson	$19.95
1067	**Madame Alexander** Dolls, Smith	$19.95
3971	**Madame Alexander** Dolls Price Guide #20, Smith	$9.95
2185	**Modern Collector's** Dolls I, Smith	$17.95
2186	**Modern Collector's** Dolls II, Smith	$17.95
2187	**Modern Collector's** Dolls III, Smith	$17.95
2188	**Modern Collector's** Dolls IV, Smith	$17.95
2189	**Modern Collector's** Dolls V, Smith	$17.95
3733	**Modern Collector's** Dolls, Sixth Series, Smith	$24.95
3991	**Modern Collector's** Dolls, Seventh Series, Smith	$24.95
3472	**Modern Collector's** Dolls Update, Smith	$9.95
3972	Patricia Smith's **Doll Values**, Antique to Modern, 11th Edition	$12.95
3826	Story of **Barbie**, Westenhouser	$19.95
1513	**Teddy Bears & Steiff** Animals, Mandel	$9.95
1817	**Teddy Bears & Steiff** Animals, 2nd Series, Mandel	$19.95
2084	**Teddy Bears, Annalee's & Steiff** Animals, 3rd Series, Mandel	$19.95
1808	Wonder of **Barbie**, Manos	$9.95
1430	World of **Barbie** Dolls, Manos	$9.95

TOYS, MARBLES & CHRISTMAS COLLECTIBLES

3427	**Advertising Character** Collectibles, Dotz	$17.95
2333	Antique & Collector's **Marbles**, 3rd Ed., Grist	$9.95
3827	Antique & Collector's **Toys**, 1870–1950, Longest	$24.95
3956	Baby Boomer **Games**, Identification & Value Guide, Polizzi	$24.95
1514	Character **Toys** & Collectibles, Longest	$19.95
1750	Character **Toys** & Collector's, 2nd Series, Longest	$19.95
3717	**Christmas** Collectibles, 2nd Edition, Whitmyer	$24.95
1752	**Christmas** Ornaments, Lights & Decorations, Johnson	$19.95
3874	Collectible Coca-Cola Toy **Trucks**, deCourtivron	$24.95
2338	Collector's Encyclopedia of **Disneyana**, Longest, Stern	$24.95
2151	Collector's Guide to **Tootsietoys**, Richter	$16.95
3436	Grist's Big Book of **Marbles**	$19.95
3970	Grist's Machine-Made & Contemporary **Marbles**, 2nd Ed.	$9.95
3732	**Matchbox®** Toys, 1948 to 1993, Johnson	$18.95
3823	**Mego** Toys, An Illustrated Value Guide, Chrouch	15.95
1540	**Modern Toys** 1930–1980, Baker	$19.95
3888	**Motorcycle** Toys, Antique & Contemporary, Gentry/Downs	$18.95
3891	Schroeder's **Toys**, Antique to Modern Price Guide	$17.95
1886	Stern's Guide to **Disney** Collectibles	$14.95
2139	Stern's Guide to **Disney** Collectibles, 2nd Series	$14.95
3975	Stern's Guide to **Disney** Collectibles, 3rd Series	$18.95
2028	**Toys**, Antique & Collectible, Longest	$14.95
3975	**Zany Characters** of the Ad World, Lamphier	$16.95

JEWELRY, HATPINS, WATCHES & PURSES

1712	Antique & Collector's **Thimbles** & Accessories, Mathis	$19.95
1748	Antique **Purses**, Revised Second Ed., Holiner	$19.95
1278	Art Nouveau & Art Deco **Jewelry**, Baker	$9.95
3875	Collecting Antique **Stickpins**, Kerins	$16.95
3722	Collector's Ency. of **Compacts, Carryalls & Face Powder Boxes**, Mueller	$24.95
3992	Complete Price Guide to **Watches**, #15, Shugart	$21.95
1716	Fifty Years of Collector's **Fashion Jewelry**, 1925-1975, Baker	$19.95
1424	**Hatpins** & Hatpin Holders, Baker	$9.95
1181	100 Years of Collectible **Jewelry**, Baker	$9.95
2348	20th Century Fashionable Plastic **Jewelry**, Baker	$19.95
3830	Vintage **Vanity Bags & Purses**, Gerson	$24.95

FURNITURE

1457	American **Oak** Furniture, McNerney	$9.95
3716	American **Oak** Furniture, Book II, McNerney	$12.95
1118	Antique **Oak** Furniture, Hill	$7.95
2132	Collector's Encyclopedia of **American** Furniture, Vol. I, Swedberg	$24.95
2271	Collector's Encyclopedia of **American** Furniture, Vol. II, Swedberg	$24.95
3720	Collector's Encyclopedia of **American** Furniture, Vol. III, Swedberg	$24.95
1437	Collector's Guide to **Country** Furniture, Raycraft	$9.95
3878	Collector's Guide to **Oak** Furniture, George	$12.95
1755	Furniture of the **Depression Era**, Swedberg	$19.95
3906	**Heywood-Wakefield** Modern Furniture, Rouland	$18.95
1965	**Pine** Furniture, Our American Heritage, McNerney	$14.95
1885	**Victorian** Furniture, Our American Heritage, McNerney	$9.95
3829	**Victorian** Furniture, Our American Heritage, Book II, McNerney	$9.95
3869	**Victorian** Furniture books, 2 volume set, McNerney	$19.90

INDIANS, GUNS, KNIVES, TOOLS, PRIMITIVES

1868	Antique **Tools**, Our American Heritage, McNerney	$9.95
2015	Archaic **Indian** Points & Knives, Edler	$14.95
1426	**Arrowheads** & Projectile Points, Hothem	$7.95
1668	**Flint Blades** & Projectile Points of the North American Indian, Tully	$24.95
2279	**Indian** Artifacts of the Midwest, Hothem	$14.95
3885	**Indian** Artifacts of the Midwest, Book II, Hothem	$16.95
1964	**Indian** Axes & Related Stone Artifacts, Hothem	$14.95
2023	**Keen Kutter** Collectibles, Heuring	$14.95
3887	Modern **Guns**, Identification & Values, 10th Ed., Quertermous	$12.95
2164	**Primitives**, Our American Heritage, McNerney	$9.95
1759	**Primitives**, Our American Heritage, Series II, McNerney	$14.95
3325	Standard **Knife** Collector's Guide, 2nd Ed., Ritchie & Stewart	$12.95

PAPER COLLECTIBLES & BOOKS

1441	Collector's Guide to **Post Cards**, Wood	$9.95
2081	Guide to Collecting **Cookbooks**, Allen	$14.95
3969	Huxford's **Old Book** Value Guide, 7th Ed.	$19.95
3821	Huxford's **Paperback** Value Guide	$19.95
2080	Price Guide to **Cookbooks** & Recipe Leaflets, Dickinson	$9.95
2346	**Sheet Music** Reference & Price Guide, Pafik & Guiheen	$18.95

OTHER COLLECTIBLES

2280	Advertising **Playing Cards**, Grist	$16.95
2269	Antique **Brass & Copper** Collectibles, Gaston	$16.95
1880	Antique **Iron**, McNerney	$9.95
3872	Antique **Tins**, Dodge	$24.95
1714	**Black** Collectibles, Gibbs	$19.95
1128	**Bottle** Pricing Guide, 3rd Ed., Cleveland	$7.95
3959	**Cereal Box** Bonanza, The 1950's, Bruce	$19.95
3718	Collector's **Aluminum**, Grist	$16.95
3445	Collectible **Cats**, An Identification & Value Guide, Fyke	$18.95
1634	Collector's Ency. of Figural & Novelty **Salt & Pepper Shakers**, Davern	$19.95
2020	Collector's Ency. of Figural & Novelty **Salt & Pepper Shakers**, Vol. II, Davern	$19.95
2018	Collector's Encyclopedia of **Granite Ware**, Greguire	$24.95
3430	Collector's Encyclopedia of **Granite Ware**, Book II, Greguire	$24.95
3879	Collector's Guide to Antique **Radios**, 3rd Ed., Bunis	$18.95
1916	Collector's Guide to **Art Deco**, Gaston	$14.95
3880	Collector's Guide to **Cigarette Lighters**, Flanagan	$17.95
1537	Collector's Guide to **Country Baskets**, Raycraft	$9.95
3966	Collector's Guide to **Inkwells**, Identification & Values, Badders	$18.95
3881	Collector's Guide to **Novelty Radios**, Bunis/Breed	$18.95
3729	Collector's Guide to **Snow Domes**, Guarnaccia	$18.95
3730	Collector's Guide to **Transistor Radios**, Bunis	$15.95
2276	**Decoys**, Kangas	$24.95
1629	**Doorstops**, Identification & Values, Bertoia	$9.95
3968	**Fishing Lure** Collectibles, Murphy/Edmisten	$24.95
3817	**Flea Market Trader**, 9th Ed., Huxford	$12.95
3819	**General Store** Collectibles, Wilson	$24.95
2215	Goldstein's **Coca-Cola** Collectibles	$16.95
3884	Huxford's Collector's **Advertising**, 2nd Ed.	$24.95
2216	**Kitchen Antiques**, 1790–1940, McNerney	$14.95
1782	1,000 **Fruit Jars**, 5th Edition, Schroeder	$5.95
3321	Ornamental & Figural **Nutcrackers**, Rittenhouse	$16.95
2026	**Railroad** Collectibles, 4th Ed., Baker	$14.95
1632	**Salt & Pepper Shakers**, Guarnaccia	$9.95
1888	**Salt & Pepper Shakers** II, Identification & Value Guide, Book II, Guarnaccia	$14.95
2220	**Salt & Pepper Shakers** III, Guarnaccia	$14.95
3443	**Salt & Pepper Shakers** IV, Guarnaccia	$18.95
2096	**Silverplated Flatware**, Revised 4th Edition, Hagan	$14.95
1922	Standard **Old Bottle** Price Guide, Sellari	$14.95
3892	**Toy & Miniature Sewing Machines**, Thomas	$18.95
3828	Value Guide to **Advertising Memorabilia**, Summers	$18.95
3977	Value Guide to **Gas Station** Memorabilia	$24.95
3444	**Wanted to Buy**, 5th Edition	$9.95

Schroeder's
ANTIQUES
Price Guide

. . . is the #1 best-selling antiques & collectibles value guide on the market today, and here's why . . .

Schroeder's **ANTIQUES** Price Guide

OUR #1 BEST SELLER!

Identification & Values Of Over 50,000 Antiques & Collectibles

8½ x 11, 608 Pages, $14.95

• *More than 300 advisors, well-known dealers, and top-notch collectors work together with our editors to bring you accurate information regarding pricing and identification.*

• *More than 45,000 items in almost 500 categories are listed along with hundreds of sharp original photos that illustrate not only the rare and unusual, but the common, popular collectibles as well.*

• *Each large close-up shot shows important details clearly. Every subject is represented with histories and background information, a feature not found in any of our competitors' publications.*

• *Our editors keep abreast of newly developing trends, often adding several new categories a year as the need arises.*

If it merits the interest of today's collector, you'll find it in *Schroeder's*. And you can feel confident that the information we publish is up to date and accurate. Our advisors thoroughly check each category to spot inconsistencies, listings that may not be entirely reflective of market dealings, and lines too vague to be of merit. Only the best of the lot remains for publication.

Without doubt, you'll find
SCHROEDER'S ANTIQUES PRICE GUIDE
the only one to buy for
reliable information and values.

COLLECTOR BOOKS
A Division of Schroeder Publishing Co., Inc.